The
Mediterranean Diet UK Meal Prep Made Easy

1500 Days of Easy and Delectable Recipes and 28-Day Meal Plan Using the Metric Measurements to Ignite Your Cooking Passion / Full Color Edition

Virginia A. Evans

Editor: AALIYAH LYONS

Interior Design: BROOKE WHITE

Cover Art: DANIELLE REES

Food stylist: SIENNA ADAMS

Table Of Contents

Introduction

Welcome to the captivating world of Mediterranean cuisine, where the rich tapestry of flavors, colors, and aromas harmoniously blend to create a symphony for the senses. In this Mediterranean meal prep cookbook, we embark on a delightful culinary journey that transcends borders and brings the vibrant tastes of the Mediterranean to the comfort of your UK kitchen.

Mediterranean cuisine has long been celebrated for its healthful benefits and delightful tastes. With a focus on fresh, seasonal ingredients, simple yet elegant cooking techniques, and a delightful array of herbs and spices, this cuisine perfectly embodies the essence of a balanced and wholesome lifestyle. Whether you are a seasoned cook or a novice in the kitchen, these pages are an invitation to explore the diversity and versatility of Mediterranean meal prep, providing you with the tools to create satisfying, nourishing, and utterly delicious dishes with ease.

Dive into the Mediterranean diet, renowned for its ability to promote longevity, heart health, and overall well-being. The foundation of this culinary tradition is rooted in an abundance of fruits, vegetables, whole grains, legumes, nuts, and seeds - all of which we will lovingly incorporate into our meal prep journey. Embrace the inclusion of olive oil, a quintessential Mediterranean staple, and let it infuse your dishes with its golden goodness, adding depth and character to every creation.

As we delve into the recipes within these pages, you will find that the Mediterranean approach to meal prep is a celebration of simplicity and taste. While we embrace the UK's dynamic food culture and adapt these recipes to local produce and preferences, we also honor the essence of the Mediterranean spirit - the joy of sharing wholesome food with loved ones and cherishing every moment spent at the table.

From light and refreshing salads that capture the essence of summer to hearty stews that warm the soul on chilly evenings, every recipe in this cookbook has been carefully curated to showcase the breadth and diversity of Mediterranean flavors. Our aim is to inspire you to experiment and explore the art of combining fresh ingredients in imaginative ways, fostering creativity in your own kitchen as you adapt these recipes to your taste and style.

Meal prep is the backbone of modern living, offering a practical solution for those leading busy lives without compromising on nutrition or taste. With the guidance provided here, you will learn to master the art of efficient meal planning, ensuring that you have a range of delectable dishes ready to enjoy throughout the week. By embracing Mediterranean meal prep, you will not only save time and energy but also elevate your everyday meals into exceptional dining experiences.

Beyond the joy of cooking, this cookbook is a celebration of the Mediterranean way of life - an invitation to slow down, savor every bite, and bask in the conviviality of shared meals. The Mediterranean culture values the precious moments spent around the table, where laughter, stories, and connections are forged, and memories are etched into the hearts of those gathered.

So, as you turn the pages and explore the recipes that lie within, we hope you embark on a culinary adventure that sparks a lifelong passion for Mediterranean flavors. May this cookbook serve as your trusted companion, guiding you through the magic of Mediterranean meal prep and inspiring you to infuse every plate with the love, warmth, and spirit of this ancient and captivating culinary tradition.

Chapter 1

Embracing the Mediterranean Lifestyle

The Development of the Mediterranean Diet

The Mediterranean diet is not a modern fad; instead, it is a culinary heritage that has evolved over centuries, shaped by the historical, geographical, and cultural tapestry of the Mediterranean region. Its roots can be traced back to the ancient civilizations that thrived along the coasts of Greece, Italy, Spain, and other Mediterranean countries. The development of this dietary pattern is a fascinating journey that reflects the profound connection between food and culture.

ANCIENT ORIGINS AND GREEK INFLUENCE

The foundations of the Mediterranean diet can be found in the diets of ancient civilizations such as the Greeks and Romans. Their culinary practices revolved around the bountiful produce that flourished in the Mediterranean climate. Grains, fruits, vegetables, olives, and grapes formed the core of their diets, and seafood was a prominent protein source due to the region's proximity to the sea. Olive oil, a symbol of prosperity and health, held a special place in both the cuisine and culture of these ancient societies.

MEDIEVAL AND ARAB INFLUENCES

As time passed, the Mediterranean diet continued to evolve through cultural exchanges and trade routes. During the medieval period, Arab influences further enriched the region's culinary traditions. Spices such as cinnamon, cumin, and coriander found their way into Mediterranean cuisine, infusing dishes with new aromas and flavors. Foods like rice, citrus fruits, and various nuts and dried fruits were introduced, adding to the diversity of the diet.

RENAISSANCE AND THE BIRTH OF ITALIAN CUISINE

The Renaissance marked a period of enlightenment and creativity, during which Italian cuisine as we know it today began to take shape. The Italian city-states, with their flourishing trade and wealth, embraced a culinary philosophy that celebrated simple and fresh ingredients. The concept of the "Mediterranean triad" - wheat, olive oil, and wine - became the foundation of Italian culinary culture. The use of herbs such as basil, rosemary, and thyme became widespread, contributing to the distinctive flavors that characterize Italian cuisine.

TRADITIONAL MEDITERRANEAN DIETS IN THE 20TH CENTURY

In the early 20th century, the Mediterranean diet began to gain attention as researchers and nutritionists recognized its potential health benefits. The Seven Countries Study, led by Ancel Keys in the 1950s, played a pivotal role in bringing the diet to the forefront of scientific research. The study found that populations in countries like Greece and Italy, where the traditional Mediterranean diet was prevalent, had lower rates of heart disease and other chronic illnesses.

MODERN RECOGNITION AND UNESCO HERITAGE

In recent decades, the Mediterranean diet has garnered international acclaim as a model for healthy eating. In 2010, UNESCO inscribed the "Mediterranean Diet" into its list of Intangible Cultural Heritage of Humanity, recognizing the diet's cultural significance and its contribution to human health and well-being. This prestigious designation further solidified the Mediterranean diet's position as a symbol of healthy living and culinary excellence.

GLOBAL SPREAD AND ADAPTATION

With the dissemination of culinary knowledge and an increased interest in health-conscious eating, the Mediterranean diet has transcended its original borders and gained popularity worldwide. People from diverse cultures have embraced the principles of the diet, adapting it to suit their regional ingredients and culinary traditions. Today, the Mediterranean diet continues to inspire chefs, home cooks, and nutritionists alike, serving as a timeless reminder of the enduring link between food and culture.

The Pillars of the Mediterranean Diet

The Mediterranean diet is more than just a collection of recipes; it is a celebration of centuries-old culinary traditions that have stood the test of time. Rooted in the sun-kissed regions that border the Mediterranean Sea, this diet embodies the art of savoring wholesome and delicious foods while fostering a deep connection with nature, community, and culture. At the heart of the Mediterranean diet lies a rich tapestry of flavors, aromas, and cooking techniques that reflect the diverse landscapes and culinary heritage of the region.

AN ABUNDANCE OF FRESH AND SEASONAL INGREDIENTS

One of the defining characteristics of the Mediterranean diet is the emphasis on fresh and seasonal produce. The region's temperate climate blesses its inhabitants with an array of fruits, vegetables, and herbs throughout the year. From ripe tomatoes and juicy citrus fruits to fragrant basil and earthy olives, these ingredients form the foundation of Mediterranean cooking, infusing dishes with vibrant colors and tantalizing flavors.

THE MAGIC OF OLIVE OIL

No exploration of Mediterranean cuisine would be complete without acknowledging the magic of olive oil. Often referred to as "liquid gold," extra-virgin olive oil is not just a cooking medium but a cherished element of the Mediterranean way of life. Its rich, fruity flavor and heart-healthy properties make it a staple in salads, dressings, and marinades, elevating the taste of even the simplest dishes.

A SYMPHONY OF AROMATIC HERBS AND SPICES

The Mediterranean is a treasure trove of aromatic herbs and spices that add depth and complexity to its dishes. Oregano, rosemary, thyme, and basil infuse Mediterranean recipes with a tantalizing medley of flavors, evoking the scents of sunlit hillsides and herb-filled gardens.

GRAINS: A FOUNDATION OF NOURISHMENT

Whole grains hold a prominent place in the Mediterranean diet, providing sustenance and a delightful chewy texture to various dishes. From nutty bulgur in tabbouleh to couscous in North African stews and the rice-based dishes of Spain and Italy, grains form a cornerstone of Mediterranean meals.

CAPTIVATING SEAFOOD AND POULTRY

Given its coastal geography, the Mediterranean diet boasts a rich assortment of seafood delicacies. Fish like salmon, sardines, and mackerel provide omega-3 fatty acids, while shellfish and mollusks lend a briny sweetness to many dishes. Poultry, such as chicken and turkey, are also celebrated for their versatility and lean protein content.

THE MEDLEY OF COLORS IN FRUITS AND VEGETABLES

In Mediterranean cuisine, a meal is often an artistic arrangement of vibrant colors. From the ruby-red hues of ripe tomatoes and bell peppers to the golden yellows of lemons and saffron, fruits and vegetables add not only taste but a visual feast to the table.

SIMPLICITY IN PREPARATION

The Mediterranean approach to cooking is characterized by its simplicity. Rather than relying on elaborate techniques or heavy sauces, the diet focuses on letting the natural flavors of fresh ingredients shine. Grilling, roasting, and sautéing with olive oil are common methods that retain the integrity of the produce while enhancing its taste.

THE RITUAL OF SHARING AND TOGETHERNESS

In the Mediterranean, meals are not just about nourishing the body but also nurturing relationships. Dining is a social affair, bringing family and friends together to share in the joy of good food and great company. The act of breaking bread is seen as a ritual of bonding and celebration, fostering a sense of community and belonging.

Health Benefits of the Mediterranean Diet

CARDIOVASCULAR HEALTH

One of the most well-documented benefits of the Mediterranean diet is its positive impact on cardiovascular health. Numerous studies have shown that following the Mediterranean diet is associated with a reduced risk of heart disease, stroke, and hypertension. The diet's emphasis on healthy fats, such as monounsaturated fats found in olive oil and omega-3 fatty acids from fish, helps lower bad cholesterol levels (LDL cholesterol) and increase good cholesterol levels (HDL cholesterol). The abundance of fruits, vegetables, whole grains, and legumes in the diet provides a rich source of fiber, antioxidants, and essential nutrients, further supporting heart health and reducing inflammation.

WEIGHT MANAGEMENT AND DIABETES PREVENTION

The Mediterranean diet has also been linked to better weight management and a reduced risk of type 2 diabetes. The diet's focus on nutrient-dense, whole foods and portion control contributes to a feeling of fullness and satiety, reducing the likelihood of overeating. Additionally, the diet's low glycemic index helps stabilize blood sugar levels, making it beneficial for individuals with diabetes or those at risk of developing the condition. The inclusion of healthy fats in the diet also aids in better insulin sensitivity, further supporting diabetes prevention and management.

BRAIN HEALTH AND COGNITIVE FUNCTION

Research suggests that the Mediterranean diet may play a role in promoting brain health and reducing the risk of cognitive decline and neurodegenerative diseases, such as Alzheimer's disease. The diet's combination of antioxidants and anti-inflammatory compounds derived from fruits, vegetables, and olive oil may help protect brain cells from oxidative stress and inflammation. Moreover, the consumption of fish, particularly those rich in omega-3 fatty acids, has been associated with better cognitive function and a decreased risk of cognitive impairment.

CANCER PREVENTION

The Mediterranean diet's abundance of plant-based foods and antioxidants may contribute to a reduced risk of certain cancers. The antioxidants found in fruits, vegetables, and olive oil help neutralize free radicals, which are unstable molecules that can damage cells and contribute to the development of cancer. Additionally, the diet's focus on fish, rather than red and processed meats, and its limited consumption of processed and sugary foods are associated with a lower risk of certain cancers, including colorectal and breast cancer.

LONGEVITY AND OVERALL WELL-BEING

Several population studies have shown that adhering to the Mediterranean diet is associated with increased longevity and overall well-being. Its nutrient-rich components provide essential vitamins, minerals, and micronutrients that support optimal bodily functions and promote overall health. The diet's emphasis on fresh and flavorful ingredients also fosters a positive relationship with food, encouraging individuals to enjoy meals with family and friends, which contributes to mental and emotional well-being.

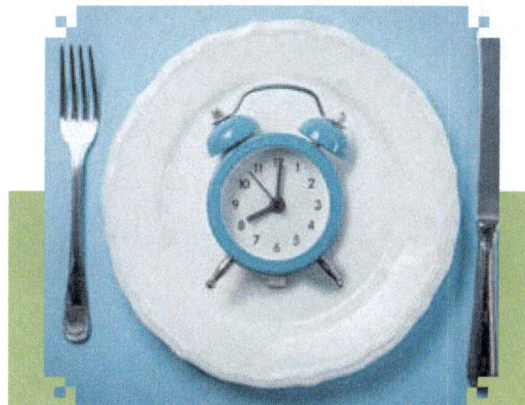

Chapter 2

The Mediterranean Pantry

The Importance of Olive Oil

Olive oil holds a central and indispensable role in the Mediterranean diet, serving as both a culinary staple and a symbol of the region's cultural heritage. For centuries, olive oil has been cherished for its rich flavor, health benefits, and versatility, making it a key ingredient in a wide range of Mediterranean dishes. Its importance in the diet extends beyond its culinary prowess; it also contributes significantly to the overall health-promoting properties of the Mediterranean way of eating.

HEART-HEALTHY MONOUNSATURATED FATS

Olive oil is predominantly composed of monounsaturated fats, which are considered heart-healthy fats. These fats have been shown to help lower bad cholesterol levels (LDL cholesterol) while increasing good cholesterol levels (HDL cholesterol). By promoting a favorable cholesterol profile, olive oil plays a crucial role in reducing the risk of heart disease and supporting cardiovascular health.

RICH SOURCE OF ANTIOXIDANTS

Extra-virgin olive oil, obtained from the first cold pressing of olives, is particularly prized for its high content of antioxidants. These powerful compounds, including polyphenols and vitamin E, help combat oxidative stress and inflammation in the body. Antioxidants neutralize harmful free radicals, which can damage cells and contribute to chronic diseases, making olive oil an essential component in promoting overall health and well-being.

ANTI-INFLAMMATORY PROPERTIES

Chronic inflammation is a contributing factor to various health conditions, including heart disease, diabetes, and certain cancers. The anti-inflammatory properties of olive oil, attributed to its polyphenols and oleic acid content, may help reduce inflammation in the body, thereby contributing to a lower risk of chronic diseases and improved overall health.

NUTRIENT ABSORPTION

The consumption of olive oil has been shown to enhance the absorption of fat-soluble vitamins, such as vitamins A, D, E, and K. When paired with vegetables or other nutrient-rich foods, the presence of healthy fats in olive oil aids in the absorption of essential vitamins, ensuring that the body receives the full spectrum of nutrients from the diet.

VERSATILITY IN COOKING

Olive oil's versatility in cooking is another aspect of its importance in the Mediterranean diet. It can be used for sautéing, roasting, grilling, and dressing salads, adding depth and flavor to a wide range of dishes. Its ability to enhance the taste of foods allows for a diverse and enjoyable culinary experience while adhering to the principles of the Mediterranean diet.

NURTURING THE MEDITERRANEAN IDENTITY

Beyond its nutritional attributes, olive oil is deeply intertwined with the cultural identity of the Mediterranean region. Olive trees have been cultivated in the Mediterranean for thousands of years, and olive oil production has been a part of the region's history and traditions. The olive tree is often regarded as a symbol of peace, prosperity, and longevity, reflecting the values that underpin the Mediterranean way of life.

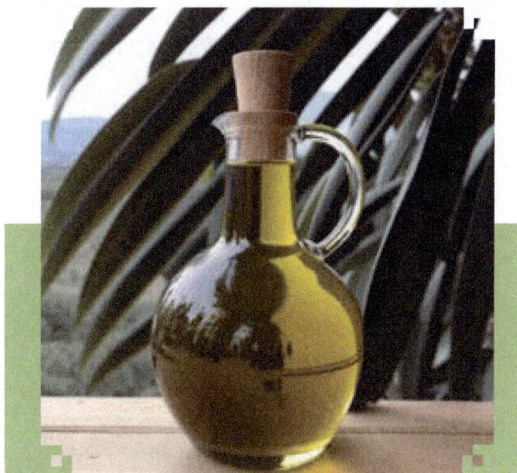

Selecting and Storing Ingredients

Selecting and storing ingredients is a crucial aspect of successful meal preparation, ensuring that the flavors and nutritional integrity of the ingredients are preserved. Whether you're following the Mediterranean diet or any other culinary tradition, here are some essential tips to guide you in selecting and storing ingredients:

FRESH PRODUCE

When selecting fruits and vegetables, opt for those that are firm, vibrant in color, and free from bruises or blemishes. Choose seasonal produce whenever possible, as it tends to be fresher and more flavorful. If buying pre-packaged produce, check for any signs of spoilage or expiration dates. Store fruits and vegetables properly in the refrigerator, as some produce may need to be kept in the crisper drawers or at specific humidity levels to maintain freshness.

GRAINS AND LEGUMES

When buying grains, such as rice, quinoa, or pasta, ensure that the packaging is intact and free from any signs of pests or damage. Store these dry ingredients in a cool, dry place in airtight containers to protect them from moisture and pests. When purchasing legumes like beans or lentils, inspect them for any foreign objects and rinse them thoroughly before cooking. Store dried legumes in sealed containers in a cool, dark pantry.

MEAT, POULTRY, AND SEAFOOD

When selecting meat and poultry, look for cuts that are fresh, well-trimmed, and free from any discoloration or strong odors. When purchasing seafood, ensure that it is firm, has a pleasant oceanic smell, and is stored at appropriate temperatures. It's best to consume fresh meat, poultry, and seafood within a few days of purchase. If not using immediately, store them in the refrigerator or freezer in airtight containers or freezer bags to prevent cross-contamination and maintain quality.

DAIRY AND DAIRY ALTERNATIVES

Check the expiration dates when purchasing dairy products like milk, yogurt, and cheese, and select those with the furthest expiration date to ensure freshness. Store dairy products in the refrigerator and maintain them at the appropriate temperature to prevent spoilage. For dairy alternatives like almond or soy milk, follow the storage instructions on the packaging and refrigerate after opening.

OLIVE OIL AND COOKING OILS

When buying olive oil, choose extra-virgin or cold-pressed varieties for the highest quality and best flavor. Store olive oil in a cool, dark place away from direct sunlight and heat to prevent oxidation. Other cooking oils, such as vegetable oil or coconut oil, should also be stored in a cool, dry place.

HERBS, SPICES, AND SEASONINGS

For dried herbs and spices, check the expiration dates and store them in airtight containers away from direct sunlight and heat to maintain their potency. Fresh herbs should be stored in the refrigerator with their stems in a glass of water, covered loosely with a plastic bag. Alternatively, you can freeze fresh herbs in ice cube trays with a little water or olive oil for later use.

By following these guidelines for selecting and storing ingredients, you can ensure that your meals are prepared with the freshest and highest-quality ingredients, enhancing the flavors and nutritional value of your dishes. Proper storage practices also reduce food waste and promote safe and enjoyable culinary experiences. Whether you're a seasoned home cook or just starting your culinary journey, paying attention to ingredient selection and storage is a valuable skill that contributes to successful and satisfying meal preparation.

Kitchen Tools and Equipment

Kitchen tools and equipment are essential components of any well-functioning kitchen, empowering home cooks to create delicious and elaborate meals with ease. From basic utensils to specialized gadgets, these tools play a crucial role in food preparation, cooking, and serving. Here are some key kitchen tools and equipment that every aspiring chef should have:

CHEF'S KNIFE

A high-quality chef's knife is a must-have tool in the kitchen. It serves as the workhorse for chopping, slicing, and dicing various ingredients. Look for a knife with a sharp, durable blade and a comfortable handle for better control and precision.

CUTTING BOARD

A sturdy cutting board provides a safe and clean surface for cutting and preparing fruits, vegetables, and meats. Opt for boards made from materials like wood or bamboo, as they are less likely to dull knife blades and are easier to sanitize.

MIXING BOWLS

A set of mixing bowls in various sizes is indispensable for combining and mixing ingredients during meal preparation. Stainless steel or glass bowls are ideal as they are easy to clean and do not retain odors or stains.

MEASURING CUPS AND SPOONS

Accurate measurements are crucial in cooking and baking. Invest in a set of measuring cups and spoons to ensure precise quantities of ingredients, resulting in consistent and delicious dishes.

WHISK

A whisk is an essential tool for blending and incorporating ingredients together, such as whisking eggs, making dressings, or creating smooth sauces.

COOKING UTENSILS

A selection of cooking utensils, including spatulas, tongs, and ladles, are essential for flipping, stirring, and serving food. Opt for heat-resistant materials like silicone to avoid damage and ensure safety during cooking.

POTS AND PANS

A well-equipped kitchen should have a variety of pots and pans for different cooking techniques. Invest in a sauté pan, saucepan, stockpot, and frying pan to cover a range of cooking needs.

BAKING SHEETS AND PANS

For baking enthusiasts, baking sheets and pans are essential for preparing cakes, cookies, and other baked goods. Non-stick or parchment-lined options make cleanup easier.

FOOD PROCESSOR OR BLENDER

A food processor or blender is a valuable tool for pureeing, chopping, and blending ingredients. It can be used for making sauces, soups, smoothies, and various culinary creations.

KITCHEN TIMER

A kitchen timer is a simple yet valuable tool for keeping track of cooking times and ensuring that dishes are not overcooked or undercooked.

GRATER AND ZESTER

A grater is handy for shredding cheese, vegetables, and spices, while a zester is perfect for adding citrus zest to dishes for extra flavor.

COLANDER

A colander is essential for draining pasta, rinsing vegetables, and straining liquids from cooked ingredients.

Chapter 3

Step-By-Step Meal Plans

Meal Plan Week 1

RECIPE NUMBER 1 - BAGUETTE BREAD

Prep time: 15 minutes | Cook time: 20 minutes | Serves: 8
Delicious on its own. Store in a paper bag or wrap in a clean kitchen towel; avoid plastic bags to maintain the crust. Consume within 2 days.

RECIPE NUMBER 2 - BEANS WITH CHICKEN SAUSAGE AND ESCAROLE

Prep time: 5 minutes | Cook time: 4 hours | Serves: 6
Serve hot and Refrigerate leftovers in an airtight container for up to 3 days.

RECIPE NUMBER 3 - ITALIAN BEEF SANDWICHES WITH PESTO

Prep time: 5 minutes | Cook time: 1 hour | Serves: 4
Assemble sandwiches with beef, cheese, pepperoncini, and pesto. Serve warm. Refrigerate any leftover beef and components separately; assemble when ready to serve.

RECIPE NUMBER 4 - LEMON COOKIES

Prep time: 10 minutes | Cook time: 10 minutes | Serves: 12
Serve as a snack or dessert. Store in an airtight container at room temperature for up to 5 days.

Week 1 Shopping List

PANTRY:
- Bread flour: (140g)
- Whole-wheat flour: (65g)
- Oat flour: (65g)
- Sugar: (1/2 teaspoon)
- Quick yeast: (3g)
- Salt: (7.5g)

GRAIN:
- All-purpose flour: (210g)

DAIRY:
- Butter, softened: (115g)
- Eggs: (5)
- Parmigiano-Reggiano cheese, coarsely grated: (60g)

FRUIT:
- Lemons: (3)

VEGETABLES, HERBS, AND SPICES:
- Garlic cloves: (2)
- Flat-leaf parsley, chopped: 4 tablespoons (2 tablespoons for the beans and 2 tablespoons for serving)
- Red pepper flakes: (1/4 teaspoon)
- Dried thyme: (1 teaspoon)
- Fresh escarole, chopped: (1 small head)
- Basil pesto: (4 tablespoons)

PROTEIN:
- Chicken sausage, cut into ¼-inch rounds: (340g)
- Beef steak, cut into strips: (680g)

CANNED GOODS:
- Cannellini beans, drained and rinsed: 1 can (425g)
- Chickpeas, drained and rinsed: 1 can (425g)
- Whole tomatoes, drained and chopped: 1 can (794g)
- Chicken stock: (360ml)

OTHERS:
- Olive oil: (25ml)
- Dry red wine: (60ml)
- Beef broth: (240ml)
- Hoagie rolls, halved: (4)
- Mozzarella cheese, sliced: (8 slices)
- Pepperoncini peppers: (120ml)
- Confectioners' sugar: (90g)

Week 1 Meal Preparation

For making Baguette bread, take a large bowl with warm water. Now sprinkle the sugar and yeast in the water and leave it for 5 minutes until it becomes foamy. Add flour and salt to the mixture and mix well. Keep mixing until it becomes a stiff dough. Take the dough and place it on a floured surface and knead until the dough becomes smooth and has an elasticity to it. Coat the insides of a bowl with oil. Shape the dough into a ball and turn the dough inside the bowl to coat it with oil. Now cover the bowl with plastic wrap and leave it in a warm place for 1 hour or until the dough doubles in size.

Mash the dough and shape it into a long slender loaf. Take a lightly greased baking sheet and place the loaf into it. Set the loaf aside for 30 minutes and in that time, preheat the oven to 450 degrees Fahrenheit. Bake the baguette in the oven for around 20 minutes or till it has a golden brown and crusty look to it. Remove the dough baguette from the oven and let it cool down before slicing.

While the dough is left for 1 hour to double in size, prepare the Beans with Chicken Sausage and Escarole. Combine the sausage, cannellini beans, tomatoes, chickpeas, and stock in a slow cooker. Sprinkle some bay leaf, red pepper flakes, thyme, 1/2 teaspoon of salt, and 1/4 teaspoon pepper. Cover it and cook over low heat for 4 hours. Put in the escarole and cook for an extra 5 to 8 minutes until wilted. Stir in the parsley and parmigiano-reggiano. For seasoning use sea salt and black pepper.

Prepare Italian Beef Sandwiches with Pesto while the chicken sausage is cooking on low heat. Take the beef cubes and season with salt and pepper. Heat olive oil in an instant pot on Sauté mode. Sear the beef until both sides are brown and it should take around 2 to 3 minutes. Add some wine to deglaze the bottom of the pot and scrape to remove any leftover beef.
Stir in the garlic powder, onion powder, oregano, and beef broth. Seal the lead on meat or stew mode for 25 minutes at high temperatures. Release the pressure after 25 minutes. Spread the bread halfway with pesto and use beef, mozzarella cheese, and pepperoncini peppers as topping.

While the Italian Beef Sandwich is on stew mode for 25 minutes, preheat the oven for Lemon Cookies. Set the oven heat at 350 degrees Fahrenheit and spray a baking sheet with nonstick cooking spray. Take a medium-sized bowl and mix cream, granulated sugar, and soften butter until it becomes fluffy. Pour in the vinegar and add egg, grated lemon zest and mix well.

Take the bowl with wet ingredients and add all-purpose flour, baking soda, and baking powder. Mix until everything is fully mixed with the dough. Place the cookie dough on the prepared baking sheet in 12 equal portions and flatten the dough with a spoon to give them a cookie shape. Bake the cookies until the edges are lightly golden, this should take 10 to 12 minutes. Do not overcook the cookies. When the cookies are baking, prepare the lemon glaze. Take a small bowl and mix the confectioners sugar, lemon juice, and grated lemon zest until it becomes a smooth batter. After baking, leave the cookies to cool down and brush the warm cookies with lemon glaze using a brush or spoon.

Meal Plan Week 2

RECIPE NUMBER 1 - RATATOUILLE WITH POACHED EGGS

Prep time: 5 minutes | Cook time: 25 minutes | Serves: 4
Serve hot with poached eggs on top. Garnish with grated Parmesan and fresh basil.
Refrigerate any leftovers in an airtight container for up to 3 days.

RECIPE NUMBER 2 - MEDITERRANEAN FRITTATA

Prep time: 10 minutes | Cook time: 15 minutes | Serves: 2
Serve warm, drizzled with olive oil. Refrigerate any leftovers in an airtight container for up to 3 days.

RECIPE NUMBER 3 - WALNUT SPAGHETTI

Prep time: 5 minutes | Cook time: 15 minutes | Serves: 6

Serve with a sprinkle of Parmesan cheese and chopped parsley. Refrigerate any leftovers in an airtight container for up to 3 days.

RECIPE NUMBER 4 - ZESTY GRILLED FLANK STEAK

Prep time: 5 minutes | Cook time: 15 minutes | Serves: 6

Slice thinly against the grain and serve. Refrigerate any leftovers in an airtight container for up to 3 days.

RECIPE NUMBER 5 - INDIVIDUAL APPLE POCKETS

Prep time: 5 minutes | Cook time: 15 minutes | Serves: 6

Serve warm. Store in an airtight container at room temperature for up to 3 days.

Week 2 Shopping List

PANTRY:

- Bread flour: (140g)
- Whole-wheat flour: (65g)
- Oat flour: (65g)
- Sugar: (1/2 teaspoon)
- Quick yeast: (3g)
- Salt: (7.5g)
- Olive oil: (60ml)
- Dry red wine: (60ml)
- Red wine vinegar: (3 tablespoons)
- Dried rosemary: (1 teaspoon)
- Dried marjoram: (1 teaspoon)
- Dried oregano: (1 teaspoon)
- Paprika: (1 teaspoon)
- Ground cinnamon: (50mg)
- Ground cardamom: (50mg)
- Nonstick cooking spray

GRAIN:

- Bread flour: (140g)

- Whole-wheat flour: (65g)
- Oat flour: (65g)
- Whole Wheat spaghetti: (500g)
- Organic puff pastry sheet

FRUIT:

- Lemons (quantity not specified)

DAIRY:

- Butter: 115g
- Mozzarella cheese: (quantity not specified)
- Soft goat cheese: (125g)
- Low-fat ricotta cheese: (2 tablespoons)
- Freshly grated, low-fat Parmesan cheese: (100g)

VEGETABLES, HERBS, AND SPICES:

- Zucchini: (454g)
- Aubergine (Eggplant): (454g)
- Onion: (1)
- Garlic cloves: (12)
- Plum tomatoes: (454g)
- Fresh basil: (15g)
- Spinach, arugula, kale, or other leafy greens: (100g)
- Quartered artichoke hearts: (113g)
- Cherry tomatoes: (16)
- Flat-leaf parsley: (2 tablespoons)
- Gala apple
- Rosemary, thyme, oregano, or basil (fresh or dried)

NUTS AND SEEDS:

- Walnuts: (150g)

PROTEIN:

- Chicken sausage: (340g)
- Beef steak: (680g)
- Flank steak: (900g)
- Large eggs: (8)

LEGUMES:

- Cannellini beans: (425g)
- Chickpeas: (425g)

OTHERS:

- Warm water: (180ml)
- Vinegar: (1 1/2 teaspoons)
- Chicken or vegetable broth: (240ml)

Week 2 Meal Preparation

For making Ratatouille with Poached Eggs, heat 1 tablespoon of olive oil in a 12-inch nonstick skillet. Heat over high heat until the oil is hot. Add the zucchini and cook for 5 minutes until it is well brown. Transfer the cooked zucchini to an empty bowl.

In the empty skillet add the aubergines, ¼ teaspoon salt, and 2 tablespoons of oil. Cook on medium heat until the aubergines turn brown and it should take about 5 to 7 minutes. Now toss the chopped onions, 1 tablespoon oil and cook for 5 minutes or until the onions are softened. Now add the minced garlic and cook for 30 seconds until fragrant. Stir the chopped tomatoes and broth and cook for 3 to 5 minutes. Now add the cooked zucchini and any accumulated juice and season with salt and pepper.

Take out the heat and make 4 shallow cuts about 2 inches wide on the surface of the ratatouille using the back of a spoon. Crack 1 egg and put into each indentation and season using salt and pepper. Cover the skillet and cook in medium-low heat until the egg whites are set and the yolk is runny, which should take about 4 to 6 minutes. Sprinkle-grated parmesan cheese and chopped basil.

While the ratatouille is cooking, preheat the oven to broiler mode over low heat for making Mediterranean Frittata. Take a small bowl and put the eggs, herbs, salt and pepper together. Whisk properly and set aside. Heat 2 tablespoon olive oil in a 4 to 5-inch oven-safe skillet on medium heat. Add the cherry tomatoes, spinach, and artichoke hearts, and sauté for 1 to 2 minutes or until everything is wilted.

Now add the egg mixture and let it cook for 3 to 4 minutes until the eggs are set. Take the goat cheese and sprinkle over the top of the egg mixture and transfer the dish from skillet to oven. Broil until the frittata is firm and the center part looks golden brown, for 4 to 5 minutes.

Take out the frittata from the oven and use a rubber spatula around the edge to loosen the sides. Now slice it in half and drizzle with 2 tablespoons of olive oil.

While the Mediterranean Frittata is in the oven, boil the spaghetti in boiling water according to the instructions for making Walnut Spaghetti. Remember to reserve 150ml of pasta water, you are going to need it later. Heat olive oil in a frying pan on medium heat. Toss in the garlic and cook until soft or about 1-2 minutes. Pour 100 ml of previously reserved pasta water in the pan and wait until the sauce is thickened, it should take 5-10 minutes. Now add the chopped walnuts and ricotta cheese and stir well until they combine properly. Drain the spaghetti and add them to the walnut sauce. Toss the spaghetti so they are well covered with walnut sauce. Add parmesan cheese and parsley on top. You can also season with salt and ground black pepper for extra taste.

Mix the ingredients for Zesty Grilled Flank Steak while the walnut sauce is thickening. Take a small bow and combine red wine vinegar, olive oil, dried marjoram, dried rosemary, paprika, dried oregano, minced garlic, and freshly ground black pepper. Now place the flank steak in a shallow dish and coat the meat thoroughly with the previously made marinade. Cover the dish and refrigerate for up to 24 hours and let the steak soak in the marinade. Take a charcoal or gas grill and preheat over 347 to 374 degrees Fahrenheit.

Now grill the marinated flank steak and turn once halfway through the cooking time to ensure even cooking. Cook the steak for 18 to 21 minutes. Make sure to check the internal temperature of the meat with a thermometer and it should be 135 to 140 degrees Fahrenheit. Now transfer the steak to a cutting board and cover with aluminum foil and leave it for 10 minutes. After 10 minutes, cut the steak into very thin slices.

While the flank steak is left to marinade, preheat the oven to 250 degrees Fahrenheit for making Individual Apple Pockets. Take the pastry dough and cut it into 4 equal dice. Peel and slice the apples and put them into a bowl. Now add brown sugar, cinnamon, and cardamom to the bowl. Take a muffin tray and spray it with nonstick cooking spray. After spraying, line the bottom of the muffin tin with the dough and place 1 or 2 broken apple slices on top. Fold the remaining dough over the apple and drizzle with honey. Bake until brown and bubbly for 15 minutes and they are good to eat.

Meal Plan Week 3

RECIPE NUMBER 1 - FALAFEL

Prep time: 5 minutes | Cook time: 20 minutes | Serves: 6
Serve with pita, tahini sauce, and fresh vegetables. Refrigerate any leftovers in an airtight container for up to 3 days.

RECIPE NUMBER2 - STEAMED MEDITERRANEAN COD

Prep time: 5 minutes | Cook time: 20 minutes | Serves: 4
Serve hot over zucchini noodles or sautéed greens. Refrigerate any leftovers in an airtight container for up to 3 days.

RECIPE NUMBER 3 - STUFFED PORK LOIN WITH SUN-DRIED TOMATO

Prep time: 15 minutes | Cook time: 30-40 minutes | Serves: 6
Slice and serve with Zucchini Noodles or sautéed greens. Refrigerate any leftovers in an airtight container for up to 3 days.

RECIPE NUMBER 4- VANILLA BITES

Prep time: 10 minutes | Cook time: 45 minutes

| Makes: 24 bites
Serve as a dessert or snack. Store in an airtight container at room temperature for up to 5 days.

Week 3 Shopping List

PANTRY:
- Dried chickpeas: (340g)
- Salt: (45g)
- Pepper
- Ground cumin: (1/2 teaspoon)
- Ground cinnamon: (1/8 teaspoon)
- Vegetable oil: (2 liters)
- Olive oil
- White rice: (240g)
- Pickled capers: (30ml)
- Ground black pepper: (1 pinch)
- Cooking twine

GRAIN:
- Butter cake mix: (340g)

DAIRY:
- Goat cheese: (240ml) crumbled
- Cream cheese: (225g) (1 package)
- Eggs: (6 large)

VEGETABLES, HERBS, AND SPICES:
- Spring onions: (10)
- Fresh parsley leaves: (1 cup)
- Fresh cilantro leaves: (1 cup)
- Garlic cloves: (7)
- Fresh thyme sprigs
- Cherry tomatoes: (454g)
- Kalamata olives: (150g)
- Sun-dried tomatoes: (2 tablespoons)
- Zucchini (optional for serving)

PROTEIN:
- Cod filets: (4)
- Pork tenderloin: (450g to 680g)

OTHERS:
- Parchment paper
- Flour (for greasing the baking pan)

Week 3 Meal Preparation

Start preparing for Falafel by dissolving 45g salt in 4 liters of cold water in a big container. Add chickpeas and let it soak for 8 to 24 hours at room temperature. Drain the chickpeas and process the chickpeas, parsley, onion, garlic, cilantro, cumin, cinnamon, 1 teaspoon salt, and 1 teaspoon pepper and process in a food processor. Process until everything is smooth or for 1 minute and scrape down everything in a bowl. Now give the chickpea mixture into 2 tablespoon size disks, making them about 1½ inches wide and 1 inch thick. Place on a parchment paper lined baking sheet.

Now preheat the oven to 392 degrees Fahrenheit. Place a wire rack on a rimmed baking sheet. Take a 12-inch frying pan and heat the oil over medium heat at 374 degrees Fahrenheit. Fry half of the falafel for about 2 to 3 minutes on each side until they are deep golden brown. Use a slotted spoon and transfer the falafel to the sheet and keep it warm in an oven. Repeat the same frying process with the rest of the falafel.

While the chickpeas are left to soak, start preparing for the Steamed Mediterranean Cod. For that, line a parchment paper on the basket of your instant pot. Place half of the tomatoes in a single layer of paper and sprinkle with thyme and reserve some for garnish. Set the cod filets on top and sprinkle some olive oil. Now take the fish and spread garlic, pepper, and salt on the fish. In the pot. Mix water and rice.

Lay a trivet over the rice and water. Lower the steamer basket onto the trivet. Seal the lid and let it cook for 7 minutes on low pressure. Remove the steam basket and trivet from the pot. You can use a fork to fluff the rice. Apply garnish of olive oil, thyme, pepper, and capers on the fish.

While the fish is cooking, preheat the oven to 250 degrees Fahrenheit for cooking Stuffed Pork Loin with Sun-Dried Tomato. Cut the cooking twine into eight 6-inch Pisces. Now cut the pork tenderloin lengthwise and leave about an inch border, remember not to cut through to the other side. Open the tenderloin like a book. Place it between two pieces of parchment paper or plastic wrap. Pound it about ¼ inch thickness. Use a meal roller, rolling pin, or the back of a heavy spoon.

Take a small bowl and combine all the goat cheese, drained spinach, chopped sun-dried tomatoes, salt, 2 tablespoon olive oil, and black pepper. Mix well so all the ingredients are combined. Spread the filling on the pork and leave a 1-inch border from long and short edges. Start rolling down the long edge and roll towards the opposite edge. To close and secure the pork, tie the cooking twine around the pork.

In a Dutch oven or a large oven-safe skillet, heat 60 ml olive oil on medium-high heat. Add the pork until all sides are brown. Remove the heat and cover the pan to bake until the pork is cooked properly. The cooking time might be different depending on the thickness of the pork, usually, it takes 45 to 75 minutes. When the pork is cooked, remove it from the oven and leave it for 10 minutes at room temperature. Slice the pork into desirable pieces and serve it over zucchini noodles or sautéed greens.

While the pork is left to cool down, preheat the oven to 350 degrees Fahrenheit for Vanilla Bites. Take a 9x13-inch baking pan and grease and flour the pan and set it aside. You can also use parchment paper. Take a medium bowl and combine butter cake mix, melted butter, and 1 egg for making the first layer. Mix all the ingredients well and make a soft dough form. Press the dough evenly into the bottom of the prepared baking pan. In another bowl, make the second layer with sugar, 2 Eggs, softened cream cheese, and vanilla extract. Mix until every ingredient is evenly combined.

Gently pour the cream cheese mixture

over the first layer. Remember to spread it evenly to cover the cake layer. Bake the vanilla bites in the oven until the top is lightly golden brown and the center is read, 45 to 50 minutes should be enough. After baking, let the cake cool down completely and cut it into 24 small square pieces to create the bites.

Meal Plan Week 4

RECIPE NUMBER 1 - CRANBERRY BREAD

Prep time: 15 minutes | Cook time: 30 minutes | Serves: 6
Serve sliced with butter or cream cheese. Store in an airtight container at room temperature for up to 3 days.

RECIPE NUMBER 2 - SHRIMP WITH MARINARA SAUCE

Prep time: 5 minutes | Cook time: 6-7 hours | Serves: 4
Serve hot over cooked spaghetti or linguine. Top with grated Parmesan cheese. Refrigerate any leftovers in an airtight container for up to 3 days.

RECIPE NUMBER 3 - BEEF SPANAKOPITA PITA POCKETS

Prep time: 5 minutes | Cook time: 15 minutes | Serves: 4
Fill pita pockets with beef mixture, Serve warm. Refrigerate any leftovers in an airtight container for up to 3 days.

RECIPE NUMBER 4 - SPANISH RICE CASSEROLE WITH BEEF

Prep time: 10 minutes | Cook time: 50 minutes
Drizzle the reduced juice syrup over the top of the filled pears, and serve hot. Store inside the refrigerator.

Week 4 Shopping List

PANTRY:

- Flour: (420g)
- Sugar: (150g)
- Vegetable oil: (160ml)
- Milk: (120ml)
- Baking powder: (2 teaspoons)

GRAIN:

- White rice (for serving): (400g)
- Long grain rice: (65g)

DAIRY:

- Eggs: (4)
- Parmesan cheese (for serving): (55g)
- Feta cheese: (60g)
- Ricotta cheese: (80g)
- Low-fat cream cheese: (120g)

FRUIT:

- Fresh cranberries: (240g)
- Firm pears: (5)

VEGETABLES, HERBS, AND SPICES:

- Garlic cloves: (8)
- Fresh flat-leaf parsley
- Dried basil: (1/2 teaspoon)
- Dried oregano: (1 teaspoon)
- Ground nutmeg: (1/2 teaspoon)
- Fresh spinach: (360g)
- Green bell pepper
- Fresh cilantro

PROTEIN:

- Cooked shrimp, peeled and deveined: (450g)
- Ground beef: (450g)
- Lean ground beef: (225g)

OTHERS:

- Olive oil: (25ml))
- Tomato paste: (170g)
- Chili sauce: (60ml)
- Worcestershire sauce: (1/4 teaspoon)
- Canned tomatoes: (1/2 can) (about 200g)
- Uncooked long grain rice: (65g)
- Ground black pepper: (1/4 teaspoon)
- Ground ginger: (1/4 teaspoon)
- Almond extract: (1/4 teaspoon)
- Sliced almonds, toasted: (30g)

- Unsalted butter (for greasing the pan)
- Cranberry juice: (240ml)
- Orange juice: (240ml)
- Pure vanilla extract: (1 tablespoon)
- Ground cinnamon: (1/2 teaspoon)

Week 4 Meal Preparation

For making Cranberry Bread combine all the ingredients in a bowl (except cranberries) and stir until well combined. Gently drop the dress cranberries into the batter and preheat the ocean to 320 degrees Fahrenheit. Take a lightly greased pan and evenly spread the mixture into it. Place the pan in the oven and bake for 30 minutes. Check with a toothpick, insert it in the middle, and see if the bread comes out clean. After baking, remove the pan from the oven and let the bread cool completely.

While the bread is baking, prepare Shrimp with Marinara Sauce. Combine all the tomato paste, minced garlic, minced parsley, dried oregano, dried basil, garlic powder, and black pepper in the slow cooker. Stir well to combine the mixture evenly. Cover and cook over low heat for 6 to 7 hours. Increase the heat to high and stir in the cooked shrimp. Cover and cook over high heat for about 15 minutes. The sauce is now ready to be served over hot cooked pasta.

While the shrimp with marinara sauce is cooking inside the oven for 7 hours, take a large skillet for making Beef Spanakopita Pita Pockets. In that skillet, heat 5 ml oil over medium heat. Add the ground beef and cook for around 10 minutes. Make sure to break it with a wooden spoon while stirring. Remove the heat and drain in a colander. Now add remeaning 10 ml oil and garlic in a skillet and cook for 1 minute. Toss the chopped spinach and cook until the spinach is ready, it should take about 2-3 minutes. Take out from the heat and mix feta cheese, ricotta, pepper, and nutmeg. Now stir until everything is evenly combined and mix the slivered almonds. The last step is to divide the beef filling among the eight pita pockets. Stuff

them well and they are ready to be served.

When the beef is cooking for 10 minutes, lightly grease an air fryer pan with cooking spray for Spanish Rice Casserole with Beef. in the greased pan add the beef and cook at 360 degrees Fahrenheit for 10 minutes. halfway through cooking, mix and crumble the beef. Now take out the extra fat and stir in the chopped bell peppers, salt, Worcestershire sauce, chili sauce, ground cumin, rice, water, brown sugar, canned tomatoes, and chopped onions. Cover the pan with aluminum foil and cook for 25 five minutes and remember to stir occasionally. After stirring, press firmly and sprinkle with shredded cheddar cheese. Bake uncovered for 15 minutes at 290 degrees Fahrenheit until the top is lightly brown. Now the dish is ready to be served.

While the beef is cooking inside the oven, peel the pears for making Cranberry-Orange Cheesecake Pears. After peeling the peers, make sure to cut a small portion from the bottom to make them sit upright. Remove the cores from the pears to create a hollow space for filling. Arrange the pears in a wide saucepan. Now, pour the cranberry juice and orange juice into the saucepan with pears. Add vanilla extract and ground cinnamon to the juice. Cook until the mixture starts to boil and reduce heat to a simmer. Cover the saucepan to let the pears simmer on low heat for 25-30 minutes or until the pears are soft but intact.

Now let the pears simmer and prepare for the cheesecake filling. Beat the softened cream cheese with ground ginger and almond extract until smooth. Stir the dried cranberries and toasted sliced almonds into the cream cheese mixture. After the pears have cooled down, spoon the cream cheese filling into the hollow pear centers. Boil the leftover juices in the saucepan until a syrupy texture. Drizzle the juice syrup over the filled pears.

Chapter 4

Breakfast and Brunch

Ratatouille with Poached Eggs

Prep time: 5 minutes | Cook time: 25 minutes | Serves 4

- 60ml extra-virgin olive oil
- 454g zucchini, cut into 2cm pieces
- 454g aubergine, cut into 2cm pieces
- Salt and pepper to taste
- 1 onion, chopped finely
- 4 garlic cloves, minced
- 454g plum tomatoes, cored and cut into 1cm pieces
- 120ml chicken or vegetable broth
- 4 large eggs
- 15g chopped fresh basil
- 28g Parmesan cheese, grated (about 120ml)

1. Heat 1 tablespoon of olive oil in a 12-inch nonstick skillet over medium-high heat until hot. Add the courgettes (zucchini) and cook until well browned, about 5 minutes. Transfer the cooked courgettes to a bowl.
2. Add the aubergines (aubergine), 2 tablespoons of oil, and ¼ teaspoon salt to the now-empty skillet. Cook over medium-high heat until the aubergines are browned, 5 to 7 minutes. Stir in the chopped onion and remaining 1 tablespoon of oil, and cook until the onion is softened, about 5 minutes. Stir in the minced garlic and cook until fragrant, about 30 seconds. Stir in the chopped tomatoes and broth, and simmer until the vegetables are softened, 3 to 5 minutes. Stir in the cooked courgettes and any accumulated juice, and season with salt and pepper to taste.
3. Off heat, make 4 shallow indentations (about 2 inches wide) in the surface of the ratatouille using the back of a spoon. Crack 1 egg into each indentation and season with salt and pepper. Cover the skillet and cook over medium-low heat until the egg whites are just set, and the yolks are still runny, 4 to 6 minutes.
4. Sprinkle with chopped basil and grated Parmesan cheese, and serve immediately.

Zesty Green Bites

Prep time: 5 minutes | Cook time: 45 minutes | Serves 8

- 50g frozen chopped kale, thawed
- 50g finely chopped artichoke hearts
- 50g ricotta cheese
- 40g grated Parmesan cheese
- 50g goat cheese
- 1 large egg white, beaten
- 1 teaspoon dried basil
- Zest of 1 lemon
- ½ teaspoon salt
- ½ teaspoon freshly ground black pepper
- 4 frozen phyllo dough sheets, thawed
- 1 tablespoon extra-virgin olive oil

1. In a bowl, combine the kale, artichoke hearts, ricotta, Parmesan, goat cheese, egg white, basil, lemon zest, salt, and pepper.
2. Place a phyllo dough sheet on a clean flat surface. Brush with olive oil.
3. Place a second phyllo sheet on top of the first and brush with more oil. Continue layering to form a pile of four oiled sheets. Working from the short side, cut the phyllo sheets into 8 strips and half them.
4. Spoon 1 tablespoon of filling onto one short end of every strip. Fold a corner to cover the filling and a triangle; continue folding over and over to the end of the strip, creating a triangle-shaped phyllo packet.
5. Repeat the process with the other phyllo bites. Place a trivet into the pot. Pour in 1 cup of water. Place the bites on top of the trivet. Seal the lid and cook on High Pressure for 15 minutes. Do a quick release.

Banana Corn Cakes

Prep time: 5 minutes | Cook time: 15 minutes | Serves 2

- 120g yellow cornmeal
- 60g flour
- 2 small ripe bananas, peeled and mashed
- 1 large egg
- 30ml milk
- 1/2 teaspoon baking powder
- 1/4–1/2 teaspoon ground chipotle chili
- 1/4 teaspoon sea salt
- 1/4 teaspoon ground cinnamon
- 15ml olive oil

1. Combine all ingredients except for the oil in a large bowl, and mix well until smooth.
2. Heat a cast-iron or nonstick skillet over medium-high heat.
3. Add the olive oil and drop the batter into the skillet using a spoon. Avoid letting the cakes touch.
4. Cook until the bottoms are golden brown, then flip.
5. Cakes are done when golden brown on both sides. Serve immediately.

Mediterranean Frittata

Prep time: 10 minutes | Cook time: 15 minutes | Serves 2

- 4 large eggs
- 4 tablespoons fresh chopped herbs, such as rosemary, thyme, oregano, or basil (2 teaspoons dried herbs)
- ¼ teaspoon salt
- Freshly ground black pepper
- 4 tablespoons extra-virgin olive oil, divided
- 100g fresh spinach, arugula, kale, or other leafy greens
- 113g quartered artichoke hearts, rinsed, drained, and thoroughly dried
- 16 cherry tomatoes, halved
- 125g crumbled soft goat cheese

1. Preheat the oven to broil on low.
2. In a small bowl, whisk together the eggs, herbs, salt, and pepper. Set aside.
3. Heat 2 tablespoons olive oil in a 4- to 5-inch oven-safe skillet or omelet pan over medium heat. Add the spinach, artichoke hearts, and cherry tomatoes and sauté until just wilted, 1 to 2 minutes.
4. Pour in the egg mixture and let it cook undisturbed over medium heat for 3 to 4 minutes, until the eggs begin to set on the bottom.
5. Sprinkle the goat cheese across the top of the egg mixture and transfer the skillet to the oven.
6. Broil for 4 to 5 minutes, or until the frittata is firm in the center and golden brown on top.
7. Remove from the oven and run a rubber spatula around the edge to loosen the sides. Invert onto a large plate or cutting board and slice in half. Serve warm and drizzled with the remaining 2 tablespoons olive oil.

Falafel

**Prep time:5 minutes | Cook time: 20 minutes |
Serves 6**

- 340g dried chickpeas, picked over and rinsed
- 10 spring onions, chopped coarse
- 1 cup fresh parsley leaves
- 1 cup fresh cilantro leaves
- 6 garlic cloves, minced
- ½ teaspoon ground cumin
- ⅛ teaspoon ground cinnamon
- 2 litres vegetable oil

1. Dissolve 45g of salt in 4 litres of cold water in a large container. Add the chickpeas and soak at room temperature for at least 8 hours or up to 24 hours. Drain and rinse well.
2. Process the chickpeas, spring onions, parsley, cilantro, garlic, 1 teaspoon of salt, 1 teaspoon of pepper, cumin, and cinnamon in a food processor until smooth, about 1 minute, scraping down the sides of the bowl as needed. Pinch off and shape the chickpea mixture into 2-tablespoon-size disks, about 1½ inches wide and 1 inch thick, and place on a parchment paper-lined baking sheet. (The falafel can be refrigerated for up to 2 hours.)
3. Preheat the oven to 200 degrees Celsius. Place a wire rack in a rimmed baking sheet. Heat the oil in a 12-inch frying pan over medium-high heat to 190 degrees Celsius. Fry half of the falafel until deep golden brown, 2 to 3 minutes per side. Adjust the burner, if necessary, to maintain the oil temperature of 190 degrees Celsius. Using a slotted spoon, transfer the falafel to the prepared sheet and keep warm in the oven. Return the oil to 190 degrees Celsius and repeat with the remaining falafel. Serve.

Carrot Bread

**Prep time: 15 minutes | Cook time: 30 minutes |
Serves 6**

- 225g all-purpose flour
- 1 teaspoon baking soda
- 1/2 teaspoon ground cinnamon
- 1/4 teaspoon ground cloves
- 1/4 teaspoon ground nutmeg
- 1/2 teaspoon salt
- 2 eggs
- 180ml vegetable oil
- 80g white sugar
- 80g light brown sugar
- 1/2 teaspoon vanilla extract
- 225g carrots, peeled and grated

1. In a bowl, mix the baking soda, flour, ground cinnamon, ground cloves, ground nutmeg, and salt.
2. In another bowl, add the eggs, white sugar, light brown sugar, vegetable oil, and vanilla extract. Beat until well combined.
3. Add the flour mixture to the wet ingredients and mix until just combined. Fold in the grated carrots.
4. Grease a baking pan that fits into the Air Fryer.
5. Press the "Power Button" of the Air Fryer and select the "Air Fry." Set the cooking time to 30 minutes and the temperature to 160°C (320°F). Press Start.
6. When the unit beeps, open the lid and carefully arrange the baking pan in the Air Fryer Basket. Insert it back into the oven.
7. Place the pan onto a wire rack to cool for about 10 minutes.
8. Carefully invert the carrot bread onto the wire rack to cool completely before slicing.
9. Cut the bread into desired-sized slices and serve. Enjoy your delicious Air Fryer Carrot Bread!

Baguette Bread

Prep time: 15 minutes | Cook time: 20 minutes |
Serves 8

- 180ml warm water
- 140g bread flour
- 65g whole-wheat flour
- 65g oat flour
- 1/2 teaspoon sugar
- 3g quick yeast
- 7.5g salt

1. In a large bowl, add the warm water and sprinkle the yeast and sugar over it. Set it aside for five minutes until it becomes foamy.
2. Add the bread flour and salt to the yeast mixture, and mix until a stiff dough forms.
3. Place the dough onto a floured surface and knead it until it becomes smooth and elastic.
4. Shape the dough into a ball and place it in a bowl coated with some oil. Turn the dough to coat it well with oil.
5. Cover the bowl with plastic wrap and let it rest in a warm place for about 1 hour or until it doubles in size.
6. Punch down the dough and shape it into a long slender loaf.
7. Place the loaf onto a lightly greased baking sheet and set it aside in a warm place, uncovered, for about 30 minutes to rise again.
8. Preheat your oven to 450 degrees Fahrenheit (approximately 230 degrees Celsius).
9. Bake the baguette in the preheated oven for about 20 minutes or until it becomes golden brown and crusty.
10. Remove the baguette from the oven and let it cool on a wire rack before slicing.

Cauliflower Pizza Crusts

Prep time: 10 minutes | Cook time: 30 minutes |
Serves 2

- 240ml cauliflower rice
- 7.5g tapioca starch
- 120g vegan grated mozzarella
- 1/8 teaspoon salt
- 1 clove garlic, peeled and minced
- 1 teaspoon Italian seasoning

1. Preheat the Air Fryer to 400 degrees Fahrenheit (approximately 200 degrees Celsius) for three minutes.
2. In a medium bowl, combine all the ingredients: cauliflower rice, tapioca starch, vegan grated mozzarella, salt, minced garlic, and Italian seasoning.
3. Divide the cauliflower mixture in half and spread each half into two pizza pans that have been lightly greased with oil.
4. Place one pizza pan in the Air Fryer basket and cook for twelve minutes. Once done, remove the pan from the basket and repeat the process with the second pan.
5. Top the cauliflower crusts with your favorite pizza toppings and cook for an additional three minutes in the Air Fryer to heat the toppings.

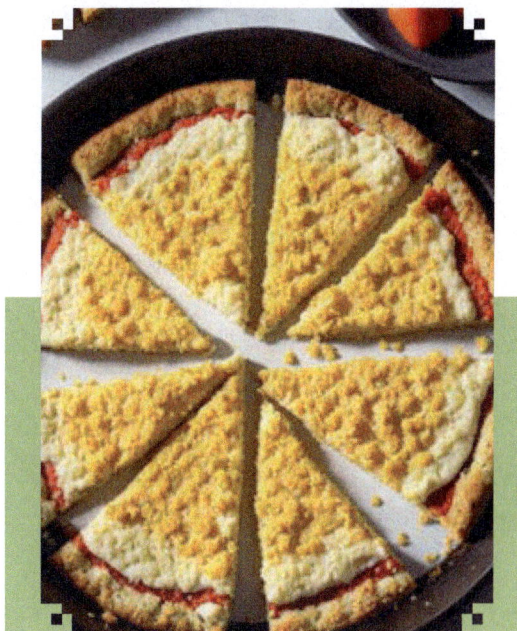

Spicy Roasted Potatoes

Prep time: 20 minutes | Cook time: 25 minutes | Serves 5

- 680g red potatoes or gold potatoes
- 3 tablespoons garlic, minced
- 1½ teaspoons salt
- 60ml extra-virgin olive oil
- 120ml fresh cilantro, chopped
- ½ teaspoon freshly ground black pepper
- ¼ teaspoon cayenne pepper
- 45ml lemon juice

1. Preheat the oven to 230°C.
2. Scrub the potatoes and pat them dry.
3. Cut the potatoes into 1.3cm (½-inch) pieces and place them in a bowl.
4. Add the minced garlic, salt, and olive oil to the potatoes, and toss everything together to evenly coat the potatoes.
5. Pour the potato mixture onto a baking sheet, spreading the potatoes out evenly in a single layer.
6. Place the baking sheet in the preheated oven and roast the potatoes for 25 minutes. Halfway through roasting, turn the potatoes with a spatula to ensure even browning.
7. Once the potato edges start to brown, remove the baking sheet from the oven and let the potatoes cool on the sheet for 5 minutes.
8. Using a spatula, transfer the roasted potatoes to a serving bowl.
9. Add the chopped cilantro, freshly ground black pepper, cayenne pepper, and lemon juice to the potatoes.
10. Toss the potatoes until all the ingredients are well mixed.
11. Serve the warm roasted potatoes as a delicious side dish to complement your meal

Cranberry Bread

Prep time: 15 minutes | Cook time: 30 minutes | Serves 6

- 4 eggs
- 420g flour
- 150g sugar
- 160ml vegetable oil
- 120ml milk
- 1 teaspoon vanilla extract
- 2 teaspoons baking powder
- 240g fresh cranberries

1. In a bowl, add all the ingredients (except the cranberries) and stir until well combined.
2. Gently fold in the fresh cranberries into the batter.
3. Preheat your oven to 320 degrees Fahrenheit (approximately 160 degrees Celsius).
4. Grease a baking pan lightly and evenly spread the mixture into it.
5. Place the pan in the preheated oven and bake for about 30 minutes or until a toothpick inserted into the center of the bread comes out clean.
6. Once baked, remove the pan from the oven and let the bread cool completely on a wire rack before slicing. Cut the bread into desired-sized slices.

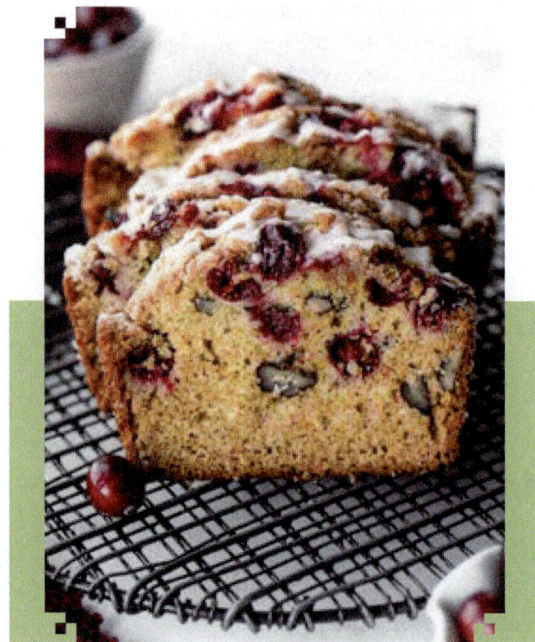

Chapter 5

Soups and Salads

Warm Spinach Salad with Feta and Pistachios

Prep time:5 minutes | Cook time: 20 minutes | Serves 6

- 45g feta cheese, crumbled
- 60ml extra-virgin olive oil
- 5cm strip lemon zest plus 30ml lemon juice
- 1 small shallot, finely chopped
- 2 teaspoons sugar
- 225g curly-leaf spinach, stemmed and torn into bite-size pieces
- 6 radishes, trimmed and thinly sliced
- 3 tablespoons chopped toasted pistachios
- Salt and pepper

1. Place the feta on a plate and freeze for 15 minutes, or until slightly firm.
2. Heat the olive oil, lemon zest, shallot, and sugar in a Dutch oven over a medium-low heat until the shallot is softened, about 5 minutes. Remove from the heat, discard the lemon zest, and stir in the lemon juice. Add the spinach, cover, and let steam off the heat until it just begins to wilt, about 30 seconds.
3. Transfer the spinach mixture and liquid left in the pot to a large bowl. Add the radishes, pistachios, and chilled feta and toss to combine. Season with salt and pepper to taste. Serve.

Seared Tuna Salad with Olive Dressing

Prep time:5 minutes | Cook time: 5 minutes | Serves 4-6

- 120g pimento-stuffed green olives, chopped
- 45ml lemon juice
- 15g chopped fresh parsley
- 1 garlic clove, minced
- 90ml extra-virgin olive oil
- Salt and pepper
- 2 (340g) tuna steaks, 1 to 1¼ inches thick
- 225g baby arugula

- 12 ounces cherry tomatoes, halved
- 1 (400g) can cannellini beans, rinsed and drained

1. Whisk the olives, lemon juice, parsley, and garlic together in a large bowl. Whisking constantly, slowly drizzle in 5 tablespoons of the olive oil. Season with salt and pepper to taste.
2. Pat the tuna dry with paper towels and season with salt and pepper. Heat the remaining 1 tablespoon of olive oil in a 12-inch non-stick frying pan over a medium-high heat until just smoking. Cook the tuna until well browned and translucent red at the centre when checked with the tip of a paring knife and registers 110 degrees (for rare), about 2 minutes per side. Transfer to a cutting board and slice into ½-inch-thick slices.
3. Whisk the dressing to re-emulsify, then drizzle 1 tablespoon of dressing over the tuna. Add the arugula, tomatoes, and beans to the bowl with the remaining dressing and gently toss to combine. Season with salt and pepper to taste. Divide the salad among plates and top with the tuna. Serve.

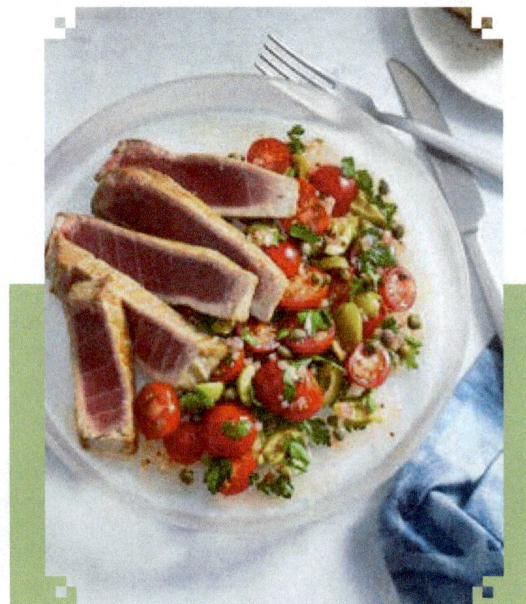

Cream of Mushroom & Spinach Soup

Prep time: 5 minutes | Cook time: 25 minutes | Serves 4

- 150g all-purpose flour
- ½ teaspoon brown sugar
- 1 teaspoon garlic powder
- 2 teaspoons dried yeast
- ¼ teaspoon salt
- 1 tablespoon olive oil
- 240ml lukewarm water
- 100g button mushrooms, chopped
- 60g Gouda, grated
- 2 tablespoons sugar-free tomato paste
- ½ teaspoon dried oregano
- 60ml lukewarm water

1. Set your Instant Pot to Sauté mode and add the olive oil and mushrooms. Sauté for 3 to 5 minutes until the mushrooms are browned on both sides. Set aside. Add the onion and spinach and cook for 3 to 5 minutes until the onion is translucent.
2. Stir in the chopped mushrooms and cook for a further 5 minutes, stirring occasionally, until golden brown.
3. Pour in the white wine to deglaze the bottom of the pot, scraping to remove any browned bits. Cook for 5 minutes until the wine has evaporated.
4. Add the remaining mushrooms, potatoes, soaked mushrooms, wine, stock, and salt. Seal the lid and cook on High Pressure for 5 minutes. Quick release the pressure.
5. Stir in the pepper and crème fraîche. Using an immersion blender, whizz the mixture until smooth. Stir in the sautéed mushrooms.
6. Garnish with the reserved mushrooms before serving.

Feta-Topped Potato Gazpacho

Prep time: 5 minutes | Cook time: 25 minutes | Serves 4

- 3 large leeks
- 3 tablespoons butter
- 1 onion, thinly chopped
- 450g potatoes, chopped
- 1.2 liters vegetable stock
- 2 teaspoons lemon juice
- 1/4 teaspoon nutmeg
- 1/4 teaspoon ground coriander
- 1 bay leaf
- 140g feta cheese, crumbled
- Salt and white pepper, to taste
- Freshly snipped chives, to garnish

1. Remove most of the green parts of the leeks, leaving the white and light green parts. Slice the leeks very finely.
2. In a large saucepan or pot, melt the butter over medium heat. Add the chopped leeks and onion to the pot and cook for about 5 minutes, stirring occasionally, until they soften without browning.
3. Add the chopped potatoes to the pot and stir well to combine with the leeks and onions.
4. Pour in the vegetable stock and add the lemon juice, nutmeg, ground coriander, and bay leaf. Season with salt and white pepper to taste.
5. Bring the soup to a boil, then reduce the heat to low. Cover the pot and simmer the soup for about 20-25 minutes or until the potatoes are tender.
6. Remove the bay leaf from the soup and discard it.
7. Use an immersion blender or transfer the soup to a blender in batches to puree it until smooth.
8. Return the pureed soup to the pot and add the crumbled feta cheese. Stir the soup until the cheese is melted and incorporated.
9. Taste the soup and adjust the seasoning with salt and pepper if needed.
10. To serve, ladle the leek and potato soup into bowls and garnish with freshly snipped chives.

Tomato Soup

Prep time: 5 minutes | Cook time: 15 minutes | Serves 6

- 30ml olive oil
- 1 large onion, coarsely chopped
- 8 large tomatoes, seeded and coarsely chopped
- 1 teaspoon paprika
- 1 teaspoon fresh ginger, finely chopped
- 1 teaspoon ground cumin
- 480ml chicken broth
- 1 cinnamon stick
- 1 teaspoon honey
- Sea salt and freshly ground pepper, to taste
- Juice of 1 lemon
- 1 small bunch flat-leaf parsley, chopped
- 2 tablespoons chopped coriander

1. Heat a large saucepan or Dutch oven over medium-high heat.
2. Add the olive oil and chopped onion, and cook until the onion becomes soft and translucent. Stir occasionally.
3. Add the chopped tomatoes, paprika, fresh ginger, and ground cumin to the pan, and stir to combine the ingredients.
4. Pour in the chicken broth, and add the cinnamon stick and honey.
5. Simmer the soup for 15 minutes, allowing the flavors to meld together. Remove the cinnamon stick from the soup before proceeding to the next step and return it when done.
6. Transfer the soup to a food processor or blender and puree until smooth. Alternatively, use an immersion blender directly in the pot to puree the soup.
7. Pour the pureed soup back into the pot, and season with sea salt and freshly ground pepper according to taste.
8. Stir in the lemon juice to brighten the flavors of the soup.
9. Serve the soup garnished with chopped parsley and coriander for added freshness and color.

Country-Style Greek Salad

Prep time:5 minutes | Cook time: 5 minutes | Serves 6-8

- 90ml extra-virgin olive oil
- 45ml red wine vinegar
- 2 teaspoons minced fresh oregano
- 15ml lemon juice
- 1 garlic clove, minced
- Salt and pepper
- 2 cucumbers, peeled, halved lengthwise, seeded, and thinly sliced
- 1 small red onion, thinly sliced
- 6 large ripe tomatoes, cored, seeded, and cut into ½-inch-thick wedges
- 1 (400g) jar roasted red peppers, rinsed, patted dry, and cut into ½-inch strips
- 100g pitted kalamata olives, quartered
- 50g chopped fresh parsley
- 50g chopped fresh mint
- 140g feta cheese, crumbled

1. Whisk the olive oil, vinegar, oregano, lemon juice, garlic, ½ teaspoon of salt, and ⅛ teaspoon of pepper together in a large bowl. Add the cucumbers and onion, toss to coat, and let sit for 20 minutes.
2. Add the tomatoes, red peppers, olives, parsley, and mint to the bowl with the cucumber-onion mixture and toss to combine. Season with salt and pepper to taste. Transfer the salad to a wide, shallow serving bowl or platter and sprinkle with feta. Serve immediately.

Panzanella Salad with White Beans and Arugula

Prep time:5 minutes | Cook time: 40 minutes | Serves 6

- 340g rustic Italian bread, cut into 1-inch pieces (4 cups)
- 75ml extra-virgin olive oil
- Salt and pepper
- 45ml red wine vinegar
- 700g ripe tomatoes, cored and chopped, seeds and juice reserved
- 1 (400g) can cannellini beans, rinsed and drained
- 1 small red onion, halved and sliced thinly
- 45g chopped fresh basil
- 30g minced fresh oregano
- 90g baby arugula
- 50g Parmesan cheese, shaved

1. Preheat the oven to 180 degrees Celsius (350 degrees Fahrenheit). Toss the bread pieces with 1 tablespoon of the olive oil and season with salt and pepper. Arrange the bread in a single layer on a baking sheet and bake, stirring occasionally, until light golden brown, 15 to 20 minutes. Let cool to room temperature.
2. Whisk the vinegar and ¼ teaspoon of salt together in a large bowl. Whisking constantly, slowly drizzle in the remaining ¼ cup of olive oil. Add the tomatoes with their seeds and juice, beans, onion, 1½ tablespoons of the basil, and 1 tablespoon of the oregano, toss to coat, and let sit for 20 minutes.
3. Add the cooled croutons, arugula, the remaining 1½ tablespoons of basil, and the remaining 1 tablespoon of oregano and gently toss to combine. Season with salt and pepper to taste. Transfer the salad to a serving platter and sprinkle with Parmesan. Serve.

Chilled Cucumber and Yogurt Soup

Prep time:5 minutes | Cook time: 5 minutes | Serves 6

- 5 large (1.5kg) English cucumbers, peeled and seeded
- 4 spring onions, green parts only, chopped coarsely
- 500ml (18fl oz) water
- 500g (1lb) plain Greek yogurt
- 1 tablespoon lemon juice
- 1½ teaspoons salt
- ¼ teaspoon sugar
- 3 tablespoons chopped fresh dill
- 3 tablespoons chopped fresh mint
- Extra-virgin olive oi

1. Toss the 5 large cucumbers (peeled and seeded) and spring onions. Working in 2 batches, process the cucumber-spring onion mixture in a blender with the water until completely smooth, about 2 minutes; transfer to a large bowl. Whisk in the yogurt, lemon juice, 1½ teaspoons salt, sugar, and a pinch of pepper. Cover and refrigerate to blend flavors, at least 1 hour or up to 12 hours.
2. Stir in the dill and mint and season with salt and pepper to taste. Serve, topping individual portions with the remaining ½-inch pieces of cucumber and drizzling with oil.

Chapter 6

Rice, Grains, Beans and Pasta

Warm Farro with Mushrooms and Thyme

Prep time: 5 minutes | Cook time: 45 minutes | Serves 4-6

- 300g whole farro
- Salt and pepper to taste
- 3 tablespoons extra-virgin olive oil
- 340g chestnut mushrooms, trimmed and chopped coarse
- 1 shallot, finely chopped
- 1½ teaspoons minced fresh thyme or ½ teaspoon dried thyme
- 3 tablespoons dry sherry
- 3 tablespoons minced fresh parsley
- 1½ teaspoons sherry vinegar, plus extra for serving

1. In a large saucepan or pot, bring 4 liters of water to a boil. Add the whole farro and 1 tablespoon of salt. Return to a boil and cook until the farro is tender with a slight chew, approximately 15 to 30 minutes. Drain the farro and return it to the now-empty pot. Cover to keep warm.
2. In a 12-inch skillet, heat 2 tablespoons of vegetable oil over medium heat until shimmering. Add the chopped chestnut mushrooms, shallot, minced thyme, and ¼ teaspoon of salt. Cook, stirring occasionally, until the moisture has evaporated, and the vegetables start to brown (about 8 to 10 minutes).
3. Stir in the dry sherry and cook, scraping up any browned bits from the bottom of the skillet, until the liquid is almost dry.
4. Add the remaining 1 tablespoon of vegetable oil and the cooked farro to the skillet. Cook, stirring frequently, until the farro is heated through (about 2 minutes).
5. Off the heat, stir in the minced fresh parsley and sherry vinegar.
6. Season the dish with salt, pepper, and extra sherry vinegar to taste.
7. Serve the British Farro with Mushrooms and Sherry in individual bowls. You can drizzle extra sherry vinegar over each serving if desired.

Parmesan Farrotto

Prep time: 5 minutes | Cook time: 30 minutes | Serves 6

- 300g whole farro
- 700ml chicken or vegetable broth
- 700ml water
- 3 tablespoons extra-virgin olive oil
- 1 onion, finely chopped
- 1 garlic clove, minced
- 2 teaspoons minced fresh thyme
- Salt and pepper to taste
- 60g grated Parmesan cheese
- 2 tablespoons minced fresh parsley
- 2 teaspoons lemon juice

1. Pulse the whole farro in a blender until about half of the grains are broken into smaller pieces, about 6 pulses.
2. In a medium saucepan, bring the chicken or vegetable broth and water to a boil over high heat. Reduce the heat to low, cover, and keep the mixture warm.
3. In a Dutch oven or large saucepan, heat 2 tablespoons of olive oil over medium-low heat. Add the finely chopped onion and cook until softened, about 5 minutes. Stir in the minced garlic and cook until fragrant, about 30 seconds.
4. Add the pulsed farro to the Dutch oven and cook, stirring frequently, until the grains are lightly toasted, about 3 minutes.
5. Stir in 5 cups of the warm broth mixture into the farro, reduce the heat to low, cover, and cook until almost all the liquid has been absorbed, and the farro is just al dente, about 25 minutes, stirring twice during cooking.
6. Add the minced thyme, 1 teaspoon of salt, and ¾ teaspoon of pepper. Cook, stirring constantly, until the farro becomes creamy, about 5 minutes.
7. Season the British Creamy Farro Risotto with salt and pepper to taste.
8. Serve the dish as a delightful and comforting main course or as a side dish.

Wheat Berry Salad with Orange and Carrots

Prep time:5 minutes | Cook time: 85 minutes | Serves 4-6

- 375g wheat berries
- Salt and pepper
- 1 orange
- 45ml red wine vinegar
- 22.5ml Dijon mustard
- 1 small shallot, minced
- 1 garlic clove, minced
- ⅛ teaspoon grated orange zest
- 1.5 teaspoons honey
- 30ml extra-virgin olive oil
- 75g peeled and shredded carrots
- 1 tablespoon minced fresh tarragon

1. Bring 4 litres of water to the boil in a Dutch oven. Add the wheat berries and 1½ teaspoons of salt, return to the boil, and cook until tender but still chewy, 60 to 70 minutes. Drain the wheat berries, spread them on a rimmed baking sheet, and let them cool completely, about 15 minutes.
2. Cut away the peel and pith from the orange. Quarter the orange, then slice crosswise into ¼-inch-thick pieces. Whisk the vinegar, mustard, shallot, garlic, orange zest, honey, and ¼ teaspoon of salt together in a large bowl until combined. Whisking constantly, slowly drizzle in the oil. Add the wheat berries, carrots, tarragon, and orange pieces and gently toss to coat. Season with salt and pepper to taste. Serve.

Orzo Salad with Arugula

Prep time: 5 minutes | Cook time: 45 minutes | Serves 4-6

- 250g orzo
- Salt and pepper
- 60ml extra-virgin olive oil, plus extra for serving
- 3 tablespoons balsamic vinegar
- 2 garlic cloves, minced
- 56g (2 cups) baby arugula, chopped
- 28g Parmesan cheese, grated (about ½ cup)
- 120ml oil-packed sun-dried tomatoes, minced
- 120ml pitted black olives (such as kalamata), halved
- 120ml chopped fresh basil
- 60ml pine nuts, toasted

1. Bring 2 quarts water to boil in large pot. Add orzo and 1½ teaspoons salt and cook, stirring often, until al dente. Drain orzo and transfer to rimmed baking sheet. Toss with 1 tablespoon oil and let cool completely, about 15 minutes.
2. Whisk remaining 3 tablespoons oil, vinegar, garlic, ½ teaspoon salt, and ½ teaspoon pepper together in large bowl. Add arugula, Parmesan, tomatoes, olives, basil, pine nuts, and orzo and gently toss to combine. Season with salt and pepper to taste. Let salad sit until flavors meld, about 30 minutes. Serve, drizzled with extra oil. (Salad can be refrigerated for up to 2 days.)

Wheat Berry Salad with Figs and Goat Cheese

Prep time: 5 minutes | Cook time: 85 minutes | Serves 4-6

- 300g wheat berries
- Salt and pepper to taste
- 2 tablespoons balsamic vinegar
- 1 small shallot, finely chopped
- 1 teaspoon Dijon mustard
- 1 teaspoon honey
- 3 tablespoons extra-virgin olive oil
- 225g figs, cut into ½-inch pieces
- ½ cup fresh parsley leaves
- 60ml pine nuts, toasted
- 60g goat cheese, crumbled

1. In a large Dutch oven, bring 4 liters of water to a boil. Add the wheat berries and 1½ teaspoons of salt. Return to a boil and cook until the wheat berries are tender but still chewy, about 60 to 70 minutes. Drain the wheat berries and spread them onto a rimmed baking sheet. Let them cool completely, about 15 minutes.
2. In a large bowl, whisk together the balsamic vinegar, finely chopped shallot, Dijon mustard, honey, ¼ teaspoon of salt, and ¼ teaspoon of pepper to make the dressing. While whisking constantly, slowly drizzle in the extra-virgin olive oil.
3. Add the cooled wheat berries, chopped figs, fresh parsley leaves, and toasted pine nuts to the dressing in the bowl. Toss gently to combine everything.
4. Season the British Wheat Berry Salad with Figs and Goat Cheese with salt and pepper to taste.
5. Transfer the salad to a serving platter and sprinkle the crumbled goat cheese over the top.
6. Serve the salad as a delightful and wholesome meal or a delicious side dish.

Lentil Salad with Olives, Mint, and Feta

Prep time:5 minutes | Cook time: 60 minutes | Serves 4-6

- 250g Puy lentils, picked over and rinsed
- 5 garlic cloves, lightly crushed and peeled
- 1 bay leaf
- 125ml extra-virgin olive oil
- 45ml white wine vinegar
- 75g pitted kalamata olives, chopped coarse
- 100g chopped fresh mint
- 1 large shallot, minced
- 20g feta cheese, crumbled (50ml)

1. Dissolve 1 teaspoon of salt in 4 cups of warm water (about 110 degrees) in a bowl. Add the lentils and soak at room temperature for 1 hour. Drain well.
2. Preheat the oven to 175 degrees Celsius. Combine the lentils, 4 cups of water, garlic, bay leaf, and ½ teaspoon of salt in a medium ovenproof saucepan. Cover, transfer the saucepan to the oven, and cook until the lentils are tender but remain intact, 40 to 60 minutes.
3. Drain the lentils well, discarding the garlic and bay leaf. In a large bowl, whisk together the oil and vinegar. Add the lentils, olives, mint, and shallot and toss to combine. Season with salt and pepper to taste. Transfer to a serving dish and sprinkle with feta. Serve warm or at room temperature.

Chickpeas with Garlic and Parsley

Prep time:5 minutes | Cook time: 20 minutes |
Serves 4-6

- 60ml extra-virgin olive oil
- 8 garlic cloves, sliced thin
- ⅛ teaspoon red pepper flakes
- 1 onion, chopped fine
- Salt and pepper
- 2 (400g) cans chickpeas, rinsed
- 250ml chicken or vegetable broth
- 2 tablespoons minced fresh parsley
- 2 teaspoons lemon juice

1. Heat 45ml of the oil, garlic, and pepper flakes in a 12-inch frying pan over medium heat, stirring frequently, until the garlic turns golden but not brown, about 3 minutes. Stir in the chickpeas and broth and bring to a simmer. Reduce the heat to medium-low, cover, and cook until the chickpeas are heated through and the flavors meld, about 7 minutes.
2. Uncover, increase the heat to high, and continue to cook until nearly all of the liquid has evaporated, about 3 minutes. Off the heat, stir in the parsley and lemon juice. Season with salt and pepper to taste and drizzle with the remaining 15ml of oil. Serve.

Cumin-Scented Lentils with Rice

Prep time: 5 minutes | Cook time: 15 minutes | Serves 2

- 60ml olive oil
- 1 medium onion, thinly sliced
- 1 tablespoon ground cumin
- 200g green lentils
- 850ml water, divided
- 150g long-grain rice, rinsed
- 2 bay leaves
- Salt and freshly ground black pepper, to taste

1. Heat a large saucepan over a medium heat.
2. Add the olive oil and onion, and cook for 10 minutes, or until soft and translucent.
3. Add the cumin and stir to combine. Add the lentils and stir to coat in the oil.
4. Add 1 pint of water, bring to the boil, then reduce the heat and simmer for 15 minutes, or until most of the water has been absorbed.
5. Add the rice to the pot, along with the remaining 0.5 pint of water and the bay leaves, and bring to the boil.

Walnut Spaghetti

Prep time: 5 minutes | Cook time: 15 minutes |
Serves 6

- 500g wholewheat spaghetti
- 100ml olive oil
- 4 garlic cloves, minced
- 150g walnuts, toasted and finely chopped
- 2 tablespoons low-fat ricotta cheese
- 100g freshly grated, lowfat Parmesan cheese
- 2 tablespoons flat-leaf parsley, chopped
- Salt and freshly ground black pepper, to taste

1. Cook the spaghetti in boiling water according to the packet instructions for al dente, reserving 150ml of the pasta water.
2. Heat the olive oil in a large frying pan over a medium heat. Add the garlic and cook for 1-2 minutes, or until softened.
3. Add 100ml of the reserved pasta water to the pan and simmer for 5-10 minutes, or until the sauce has thickened.
4. Add the chopped walnuts and ricotta cheese and stir to combine.
5. Drain the spaghetti and add it to the pan with the walnut sauce. Toss to coat.
6. Serve immediately, topped with the Parmesan cheese and parsley. Season with salt and freshly ground black pepper to taste.

Chapter 7

Poultry

Sautéed Chicken Breasts with Cherry Tomatoes

Prep time: 5 minutes | Cook time: 25 minutes | Serves 4

- 120g all-purpose flour
- 4 boneless, skinless chicken breasts, trimmed
- 1 teaspoon herbes de Provence
- Salt and pepper to taste
- 45ml plus 10ml extra-virgin olive oil
- 2 zucchini, quartered lengthwise and sliced 1 cm thick
- 2 yellow summer squash, quartered lengthwise and sliced 1 cm thick
- 2 garlic cloves, minced
- 340g cherry tomatoes, halved
- 2 tablespoons capers, rinsed
- 60ml shredded fresh basil or mint

1. Spread the all-purpose flour in a shallow dish. Pat the chicken breasts dry with paper towels, sprinkle with herbes de Provence, salt, and pepper. Working with one chicken breast at a time, dredge it in flour to coat, shaking off any excess.
2. In a large nonstick skillet, heat 45ml of extra-virgin olive oil over medium-high heat until it's just smoking. Transfer the cooked chicken to a plate, tent it loosely with aluminum foil, and let it rest while preparing the vegetables.
3. In the same skillet, heat the remaining 10ml of extra-virgin olive oil over medium-high heat until shimmering. Add the sliced zucchini and yellow summer squash to the skillet and cook until they are well browned, about 10 minutes.
4. Stir in the minced garlic and cook for an additional 30 seconds until fragrant.
5. Add the halved cherry tomatoes and capers to the skillet and cook until the tomatoes are just softened, about 2 minutes.
6. Remove the skillet from the heat and stir in the shredded fresh basil or mint.
7. Season the vegetable mixture with salt and pepper to taste.
8. Serve the herbed chicken with the sautéed summer vegetables and enjoy your delicious British-inspired dish!

Beans with Chicken Sausage and Escarole

Prep time: 5 minutes | Cook time: 4 hours | Serves 6

- 340 grams chicken sausage, cut into ¼-inch rounds
- 1 (425-gram) can cannellini beans, drained and rinsed
- 1 (425-gram) can chickpeas, drained and rinsed
- 1 (794-gram) can whole tomatoes, drained and chopped
- 360 ml chicken stock
- 1 bay leaf
- 1 teaspoon dried thyme
- ¼ teaspoon red pepper flakes
- ½ teaspoon sea salt
- ¼ teaspoon black pepper
- 1 small head escarole, chopped
- 60 ml coarsely grated parmigiano-reggiano cheese
- 2 tablespoons chopped fresh flat-leaf parsley

1. Combine sausage, cannellini beans, chickpeas, tomatoes, and stock in the slow cooker. Sprinkle on the bay leaf, thyme, red pepper flakes, ½ teaspoon salt, and ¼ teaspoon pepper.
2. Cover and cook on low for 4 hours.
3. Stir in the escarole and cook an additional 5 to 8 minutes, until just wilted. Stir in the Parmigiano-Reggiano and parsley. Season with additional sea salt and black pepper. Serve hot.

Grilled Chicken Souvlaki

Prep time: 5 minutes | Cook time: 45 minutes | Serves 4-6

- Salt and pepper to taste
- 680g boneless, skinless chicken breasts, trimmed and cut into 1-inch pieces
- 80ml extra-virgin olive oil
- 2 tablespoons minced fresh parsley
- 1 teaspoon finely grated lemon zest plus 60ml juice (2 lemons)
- 1 teaspoon honey
- 1 teaspoon dried oregano
- 1 green bell pepper, quartered, stemmed, seeded, and each quarter cut into 4 pieces
- 1 small red onion, halved through the root end, each half cut into 4 chunks
- 4–6 (8-inch) pita breads
- 240ml Tzatziki (Greek yogurt and cucumber sauce)

1. Dissolve 2 tablespoons of salt in 1 quart of cold water in a large container. Submerge the chicken in the brine, cover, and refrigerate for 30 minutes.
2. In a medium bowl, combine the extra-virgin olive oil, minced fresh parsley, finely grated lemon zest, lemon juice, honey, oregano, and black pepper to make the Lemon-Honey Dressing. Reserve ¼ cup of the dressing in a large bowl.
3. Remove the chicken from the brine and pat it dry with paper towels. Toss the chicken with the remaining oil mixture.
4. Thread 4 pieces of bell pepper, concave side up, onto one 12-inch metal skewer. Thread one-quarter of the chicken onto the same skewer. Thread 2 chunks of onion onto the skewer and place it on a plate. Repeat the skewering process with the remaining chicken and vegetables on 3 more skewers.
5. Lightly moisten 2 pita breads with water. Sandwich the unmoistened pitas between the moistened ones and wrap the stack tightly in lightly greased heavy-duty aluminum foil.
6. Heat the grill (either charcoal or gas) until hot.
7. Clean and oil the cooking grate. Place the skewers on the hotter side of the grill and cook, turning occasionally, until the chicken and vegetables are well browned and the chicken reaches an internal temperature of 160°F (71°C), which should take about 15 to 20 minutes.
8. Using tongs, slide the chicken and vegetables off the skewers into the bowl of reserved oil mixture. Toss gently, breaking up the onion chunks. Cover loosely with foil and let it sit while heating the pitas.
9. Place the packet of pitas on the cooler side of the grill and flip them occasionally until heated through, about 5 minutes.
10. Lay each warm pita on a 12-inch square of foil. Spread each pita with 2 tablespoons of Tzatziki. Place one-quarter of the chicken and vegetables in the middle of each pita. Roll into a cylindrical shape and serve.

Quinoa Chicken Chili

Prep time: 10 minutes | Cook time:5 to 7 hours |Serves 8

- 1 teaspoon olive oil
- 1/2 onion, minced
- 2 cloves garlic, minced
- 2 large boneless, skinless chicken breasts, diced
- 1 cup quinoa, rinsed
- 1 (400g) can crushed tomatoes
- 1 (400g) can diced tomatoes with green chillies
- 2 (400g) cans black beans, drained and rinsed
- 2 (400g) cans corn kernels, fresh or frozen and thawed
- 1 large bell pepper, any colour, chopped
- 625ml chicken stock
- 1 teaspoon ground cumin
- 1 teaspoon red pepper flakes
- 1 teaspoon chilli powder
- 1/2 teaspoon sea salt
- 1/2 teaspoon black pepper
- 1 x 225g tub plain Greek yogurt, for serving (optional)
- 50g grated Parmesan cheese, for serving (optional)

1. Heat the olive oil over a medium heat in a medium frying pan. Add the onion and garlic and cook for 1 minute.
2. Add the chicken to the pan and cook until browned, about 5 minutes. Transfer the chicken to the slow cooker.
3. To the slow cooker, add the quinoa, crushed tomatoes, diced tomatoes with chillies, black beans, corn, bell pepper, and chicken stock. Sprinkle in the cumin, red pepper flakes, chilli powder, 1/2 teaspoon salt, and 1/2 teaspoon pepper.
4. Cover and cook on low for 5 to 7 hours. Remove the chicken, shred it, and return it to the slow cooker. Season with more salt and pepper, if necessary. Keep warm until ready to serve.
5. For serving, garnish with Greek yogurt and/or Parmesan, if desired.

Rice and Turkey Slow Cooker Bake

Prep time: 10 minutes | Cook time:6 to 8 hours |Serves 6

- Nonstick cooking oil spray
- 680 grams ground turkey
- 1 teaspoon sea salt
- ½ teaspoon black pepper
- 2 tablespoons chopped fresh thyme
- 2 tablespoons chopped fresh sage
- 360 grams converted brown rice
- 480 ml chicken stock (or turkey stock if you have it)
- 1 tablespoon plus 1 teaspoon balsamic vinegar
- 1 medium yellow onion, chopped
- 2 garlic cloves, minced
- One 400-gram can stewed tomatoes, with the juice
- 3 medium-size zucchini, sliced thinly
- 60 ml pitted and sliced kalamata olives
- 60 ml chopped fresh flat-leaf parsley
- 120 ml grated parmigiano-reggiano cheese, for serving (optional)

1. Spray a large skillet with cooking oil spray. Place over medium-high heat. Add the ground turkey, 1 teaspoon salt, ½ teaspoon pepper, 1 tablespoon of the thyme, and 1 tablespoon of the sage. Sauté until turkey is no longer pink. Drain off the fat, and place the turkey mixture into the slow cooker.
2. Add the rice, chicken stock, and vinegar and stir to combine. Add the onion, garlic, tomatoes, zucchini, and olives and stir. Add the remaining 1 tablespoon thyme, remaining 1 tablespoon sage, and parsley. Mix well.
3. Cover and cook on low for 6 to 8 hours, or on high for 3 to 4 hours.
4. Season with additional salt and pepper if needed. Serve hot with Parmigiano-Reggiano cheese sprinkled on top, if desired.

Roasted Chicken Thighs with Fennel

Prep time: 5 minutes | Cook time: 40 minutes | Serves 8

- 3 shallots, sliced thinly (about ½ cup)
- 5 tablespoons extra-virgin olive oil
- 8 bone-in chicken thighs (about 5-7 ounces each), trimmed
- Salt and pepper
- 45g fresh parsley leaves
- 60ml pitted oil-cured black olives, chopped
- 60ml water
- 2 teaspoons red wine vinegar
- 1 anchovy fillet, rinsed
- 1 teaspoon grated orange zest
- ½ teaspoon ground fennel seeds
- ¼ teaspoon red pepper flakes

1. Adjust the oven racks to the middle and lowest positions. Place a rimmed baking sheet on the lower rack and preheat the oven to 230°C.
2. In a bowl, toss the shallots with 1 tablespoon of olive oil. Cover the bowl and microwave until the shallots have softened, about 3 minutes, stirring once halfway through microwaving. Place the shallots in the center of a 12-inch square of aluminum foil. Cover with a second 12-inch square of foil and fold the edges together to create a packet about 7 inches square. Set the packet aside.
3. Using a metal skewer, poke the skin side of the chicken thighs 10 to 12 times. Pat the thighs dry with paper towels, then rub the skin with 1 tablespoon of olive oil and season with salt and pepper. Place the thighs skin side down on the hot baking sheet and place the foil packet on the upper rack of the oven. Roast the chicken until the skin side is beginning to brown and the internal temperature reaches 71°C (160°F), which should take about 17 to 22 minutes, rotating the sheet and removing the foil packet after 10 minutes. Remove the chicken from the oven and preheat the broiler.
4. Flip the chicken thighs skin side up and broil on the upper rack until the skin is crisp and well browned, and the internal temperature reaches 79°C, about 5 minutes, rotating the sheet as needed for even browning. Transfer the chicken to a serving platter and let it rest while preparing the sauce.
5. In a food processor, pulse the shallots, parsley, olives, water, red wine vinegar, rinsed anchovy fillet, grated orange zest, ground fennel seeds, red pepper flakes, and ¼ teaspoon of salt until finely chopped, about 10 pulses. With the processor running, slowly drizzle in the remaining 3 tablespoons of olive oil and process until incorporated, scraping down the sides of the bowl as needed. Season the sauce with salt and pepper to taste.
6. Serve the British-style Roasted Chicken with Olive-Parsley Sauce, drizzling the flavorful sauce over the chicken just before serving.

Cheesy Chicken Omelet

Prep time: 5 minutes | Cook time: 18 minutes | Serves 2

- half cup cooked Chicken Breast, (diced) divided
- Four eggs
- 1/4 tsp onion powder, divided
- 50mg salt, divided
- 1/4 tsp. pepper, divided
- 30g shredded cheese, divided
- 25ml garlic powder, divided

1. Take two ramekins and grease them with olive oil.
2. Add two eggs to each ramekin. Then, add cheese with seasoning.
3. Blend to combine. Add 1/4 cup of cooked chicken on top.
4. Cook for 18 minutes in the Air Fryer at 165°C.

Chapter 8

Pork, Beef and Lamb

Pork Chops & Broccoli with Gravy

Prep time: 5 minutes | Cook time: 45 minutes | Serves 6

Pork Chops:

- 1 ½ teaspoons salt
- 1 teaspoon ground black pepper
- 1 teaspoon garlic powder
- 1 teaspoon onion powder
- 1 teaspoon red pepper flakes
- 6 boneless pork chops
- 1 broccoli head, broken into florets
- 240ml chicken stock
- 60g butter, melted
- 60ml milk

Gravy:

- 3 tablespoons flour
- 120ml double cream (heavy cream)
- Salt and ground black pepper to taste

1. Combine salt, garlic powder, flakes, onion, and black pepper. Rub the mixture onto pork chops. Place stock and broccoli in the instant pot. Lay the pork chops on top.
2. 2.Seal the lid and cook for 15 minutes on High Pressure. Release the Pressure quickly.
3. 3.Transfer the pork chops and broccoli to a plate. Press Sauté and simmer the liquid remaining in the pot.
4. 4.Mix cream and flour. Pour into the simmering liquid and cook for 4 to 6 minutes until thickened and bubbly. Season with pepper and salt. Top the chops with gravy, drizzle butter over broccoli and serve.

Grilled Flank Steak with Grilled Vegetables

Prep time: 5 minutes | Cook time: 35 minutes | Serves 4-6

- 1 red onion, sliced into 1.25 cm-thick rounds
- 350g cherry tomatoes
- 2 zucchini, sliced lengthwise into 2 cm-thick planks
- 1 pound aubergine, sliced lengthwise into 2 cm-thick planks
- 2 tablespoons extra-virgin olive oil
- 680g flank steak, trimmed
- Salt and pepper to taste
- 120ml Italian Green Sauce (Salsa Verde)

1. Thread the onion rounds from side to side onto two 30cm metal skewers. Thread the cherry tomatoes onto two 30cm metal skewers. Brush the onion rounds, tomatoes, zucchini, and aubergine with oil and season with salt and pepper. Pat the flank steak dry with paper towels and season with salt and pepper.
2. For a charcoal grill: Open the bottom grill vent completely. Light a large chimney starter filled with charcoal briquettes (about 6 quarts). When the top coals are partially covered with ash, pour them evenly over the grill. Set the cooking grate in place, cover the grill, and open the lid vent completely. Heat the grill until hot, about 5 minutes.
3. For a gas grill: Turn all burners to high, cover the grill, and heat it until hot, about 15 minutes. Leave all burners on high.
4. Clean and oil the cooking grate. Place the steak, onion, and tomato skewers, zucchini, and aubergine on the grill. Cook (covered if using gas), flipping the steak and turning the vegetables as needed, until the steak is well browned and reaches an internal temperature of 120 to 125 degrees Fahrenheit (for medium-rare) and the vegetables are slightly charred and tender, which should take about 7 to 12 minutes. Transfer the steak and vegetables to a carving board as they finish grilling and tent loosely with aluminum foil. Let the steak rest for 10 minutes.

Stuffed Pork Loin with Sun-Dried Tomato

Prep time: 15 minutes | Cook time:30 to 40 minutes |Serves 6

- 450g to 680g pork tenderloin
- 240ml crumbled goat cheese
- 115g frozen spinach, thawed and well-drained
- 2 tablespoons chopped sun-dried tomatoes
- 2 tablespoons extra-virgin olive oil (or seasoned oil marinade from sun-dried tomatoes), plus 60ml, divided
- 1/2 teaspoon salt
- 1/2 teaspoon freshly ground black pepper
- Zucchini Noodles or sautéed greens, for serving

1. Preheat the oven to 180°C (350°F). Cut cooking twine into eight (6-inch) pieces.
2. Cut the pork tenderloin in half lengthwise, leaving about an inch border, being careful not to cut all the way through to the other side. Open the tenderloin like a book to form a large rectangle. Place it between two pieces of parchment paper or plastic wrap and pound it to about 1/4-inch thickness using a meat mallet, rolling pin, or the back of a heavy spoon.
3. In a small bowl, combine the goat cheese, thawed and drained spinach, chopped sun-dried tomatoes, 2 tablespoons of olive oil, salt, and black pepper. Mix well to incorporate all the ingredients.
4. Spread the filling over the surface of the pork, leaving a 1-inch border from one long edge and both short edges. To roll, start from the long edge with the filling and roll towards the opposite edge. Tie cooking twine around the pork to secure it closed, evenly spacing each of the eight pieces of twine along the length of the roll.
5. In a Dutch oven or large oven-safe skillet, heat 60ml of olive oil over medium-high heat. Add the pork and brown it on all sides. Then, remove the pork from the heat, cover the pan, and bake until the pork is cooked through. The cooking time will vary depending on the thickness of the pork, but it usually takes 45 to 75 minutes.
6. Once the pork is cooked, remove it from the oven and let it rest for 10 minutes at room temperature.
7. To serve, remove the twine and discard it. Slice the pork into medallions and serve it over Zucchini Noodles or sautéed greens, spooning the cooking oil and any bits of filling that fell out during cooking over the top.

Italian Beef Sandwiches with Pesto

Prep time: 5 minutes | Cook time: 1 hour | Serves 4

- 680g beef steak, cut into strips
- Salt and ground black pepper
- 15ml olive oil
- 60ml dry red wine
- 240ml beef broth
- 15ml oregano
- 5ml onion powder
- 5ml garlic powder
- 4 hoagie rolls, halved
- 8 slices mozzarella cheese
- 120ml pepperoncini peppers
- 4 tablespoons pesto

1. Season the beef cubes with salt and pepper. Heat the olive oil in your Instant Pot on Sauté mode. Sear the beef for 2 to 3 minutes per side until browned. Add the wine to deglaze the bottom of the pot, scraping to remove any browned bits of beef. Stir in the garlic powder, beef broth, onion powder, and oregano.
2. Seal the lid and cook on Meat/Stew mode for 25 minutes on High. Quick release the pressure.
3. Spread each bread half with pesto. Top with the beef, pepperoncini peppers, and mozzarella cheese. Close the sandwiches and serve.

Peppery Beef

Prep time: 5 minutes | Cook time: 45 minutes | Serves 6

- 900 grams lean beef, cut into bite-sized pieces
- 5 onions, peeled and chopped
- 5 garlic cloves, peeled and crushed
- 1 teaspoon salt
- 1 jalapeno pepper, deseeded and chopped
- 1 bell pepper, deseeded and chopped
- Freshly ground black pepper, to taste
- 1 teaspoon cayenne pepper
- 2 tablespoons tomato purée
- 5ml tablespoons vegetable oil

1. Heat the vegetable oil on the "Sauté" setting. Stir-fry the chopped onions and crushed garlic for 2-3 minutes until softened.
2. Add the bite-sized pieces of lean beef to the pot, along with the salt, black pepper, cayenne pepper, and tomato purée. Mix well to coat the beef with the spices and sauce.
3. Pour enough water into the pot to cover the ingredients. Seal the lid of the pressure cooker and cook on "High Pressure" for 20 minutes.
4. Once the cooking time is complete, perform a quick pressure release to release the pressure from the pot.

Beef and Wild Mushroom Stew

Prep time: 5 minutes | Cook time: 15 minutes | Serves 8

- 900g fresh porcini or morel mushrooms, trimmed and sliced
- 60ml olive oil
- 900g lean, boneless beef, cut into 2-inch cubes
- 2 large onions, finely chopped
- 2 cloves garlic, minced
- 240ml dry white wine

- 1 teaspoon dried thyme
- 1 teaspoon sea salt
- 1/2 teaspoon freshly ground black pepper

1. Heat the olive oil in a large heavy-bottomed casserole dish over a medium heat. Add the beef and brown all over, about 5 minutes per side. Remove the beef from the pan and set aside.
2. Add the onions and garlic to the pan and cook for 5 minutes, or until softened.
3. Add the mushrooms to the pan and cook for 10 minutes, or until softened and lightly browned.
4. Return the beef to the pan and add the white wine, thyme, salt, and pepper. Bring to a boil, then reduce heat to low, cover, and simmer for 1 hour, or until the beef is tender.

Yogurt-and-Herb-Marinated Pork Tenderloin

Prep time: 5 minutes | Cook time: 25 minutes| Serves 6

- Nonstick cooking spray
- 2 medium pork tenderloins (280-340g each)
- ½ teaspoon freshly ground black pepper
- ½ teaspoon kosher or sea salt
- 60ml 2% plain Greek yogurt
- 15ml chopped fresh rosemary
- Tzatziki yogurt sauce from Chickpea Patties in Pitas (here, step 3) or store-bought tzatziki sauce
- 1 to 2 tablespoons chopped fresh mint (optional)

1. Preheat the oven to 260°C.
2. Line a large, rimmed baking sheet with aluminum foil. Place a wire cooling rack on the aluminum foil, and spray the rack with nonstick cooking spray.
3. Place both pieces of the pork on the wire rack, folding under any skinny ends of the meat to ensure even cooking. Sprinkle both pieces evenly with the pepper and salt.

Zesty Grilled Flank Steak

Prep time: 5 minutes | Cook time: 15 minutes | Serves 6

- 60ml olive oil
- 3 tablespoons red wine vinegar
- 1 teaspoon dried rosemary
- 1 teaspoon dried marjoram
- 1 teaspoon dried oregano
- 1 teaspoon paprika
- 2 cloves garlic, minced
- 1 teaspoon freshly ground black pepper
- 900g beef flank steak

1. In a small bowl, combine the olive oil, red wine vinegar, dried rosemary, dried marjoram, dried oregano, paprika, minced garlic, and freshly ground pepper to create the marinade.
2. Place the flank steak in a shallow dish and rub the marinade thoroughly into the meat. Cover the dish and refrigerate for up to 24 hours to marinate the steak.
3. Preheat a charcoal or gas grill to medium heat (approximately 175–190 degrees Celsius).
4. Grill the marinated flank steak for 18–21 minutes, turning it once halfway through the cooking time to ensure even cooking.
5. Check the internal temperature of the meat with a meat thermometer, and it should read 135–140 degrees Fahrenheit (approximately 57–60 degrees Celsius) when the steak is done to your desired level of doneness.
6. Transfer the grilled steak to a cutting board and cover it with aluminum foil. Allow the steak to rest for at least 10 minutes before slicing.
7. Slice the steak very thinly against the grain and serve.

Spanish Rice Casserole with Beef

Prep time: 10 Minutes | Cook time: 50 minutes | Serves 3

- 225g lean ground beef
- 2 tablespoons chopped green bell pepper
- 1 tablespoon chopped fresh cilantro
- 30g shredded Cheddar cheese
- 1/2 teaspoon brown sugar
- 1/2 pinch ground pepper
- 65g uncooked long grain rice
- 30g finely chopped onion
- 60ml chili sauce
- 1/4 teaspoon ground cumin
- 1/4 teaspoon Worcestershire sauce
- 1/2 (200g) can of canned tomatoes
- 120ml water
- 1/2 teaspoon salt

1. Lightly grease the Air Fryer pan with cooking spray. Add the ground beef.
2. Cook at 180°C (360°F) for ten minutes. Halfway through cooking, mix and crumble the beef.
3. Discard excess fat and stir in chopped green bell pepper, Worcestershire sauce, salt, chili sauce, rice, ground cumin, brown sugar, water, canned tomatoes, and chopped onion. Cover the pan with aluminum foil and cook for twenty-five minutes, stirring occasionally.
4. Give one last good stir, press firmly, and sprinkle with shredded Cheddar cheese.
5. Bake uncovered for fifteen minutes at 200°C (390°F) until the tops are lightly browned.
6. Serve with chopped fresh cilantro. Enjoy your flavorful Air Fryer Beef and Rice Casserole!

Beef Spanakopita Pita Pockets

Prep time: 5 minutes | Cook time: 15 minutes|
Serves 4

- 15ml extra-virgin olive oil, divided
- 450g ground beef (93% lean)
- 2 garlic cloves, minced (about 1 teaspoon)
- 2 (170g) bags baby spinach, chopped (about 360g)
- 60g crumbled feta cheese (about 60g)
- 80g ricotta cheese
- ½ teaspoon ground nutmeg
- ¼ teaspoon freshly ground black pepper
- 30g slivered almonds
- 4 whole-wheat pita breads, cut in half

1. In a large skillet over medium heat, heat 5ml of oil. Add the ground beef and cook for 10 minutes, breaking it up with a wooden spoon and stirring occasionally. Remove from the heat and drain in a colander. Set the meat aside.
2. Place the skillet back on the heat, and add the remaining 10ml of oil. Add the garlic and cook for 1 minute, stirring constantly. Add the chopped spinach and cook for 2 to 3 minutes, or until the spinach has cooked down, stirring often.
3. Turn off the heat and mix in the feta cheese, ricotta, nutmeg, and pepper. Stir until all the ingredients are well incorporated. Mix in the slivered almonds.
4. Divide the beef filling among the eight pita pocket halves to stuff them and serve.

Beef & Rice Stuffed Onions

Prep time: 5 minutes | Cook time: 30 minutes |
Serves 4

- 10 small sweet onions, peeled
- 450g lean minced beef
- 125g rice
- 45ml olive oil
- 15ml ground mint
- 5ml ground cayenne pepper
- 2.5ml ground cumin
- 5ml salt
- 7.5ml tomato paste
- 60g bread crumbs
- A handful of fresh parsley, finely chopped
- Sour cream, for serving
- Pide bread or any other flatbread, for serving

1. Cut a ¼-inch slice from the top of each onion and trim a small amount from the bottom end, this will make the onions stand upright. Place the onions in a microwave-safe dish and pour 1 cup of water over them. Cover with a tight lid and microwave for 10-12 minutes, or until the onions soften. Remove the onions and cool slightly. Carefully remove the inner layers of the onions with a paring knife, leaving about a ¼-inch onion shell.
2. In a bowl, combine the ground beef, rice, olive oil, mint, cayenne pepper, cumin, salt, and bread crumbs. Use 1 tablespoon of the mixture to fill each onion.
3. Grease the inner pot of your Instant Pot with oil. Add the onions and pour 2.5 cups of water into the pot.
4. Seal the lid and cook on Manual/ Pressure Cook mode for 10 minutes on High. Quick release the pressure.
5. Top the stuffed onions with parsley and serve with sour cream and pide bread.

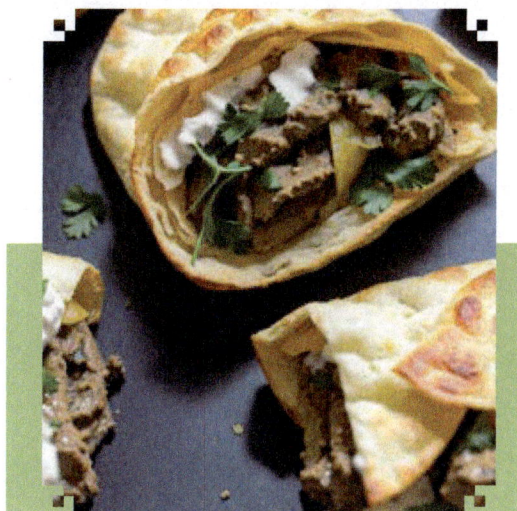

Chapter 9

Fish and Seafood

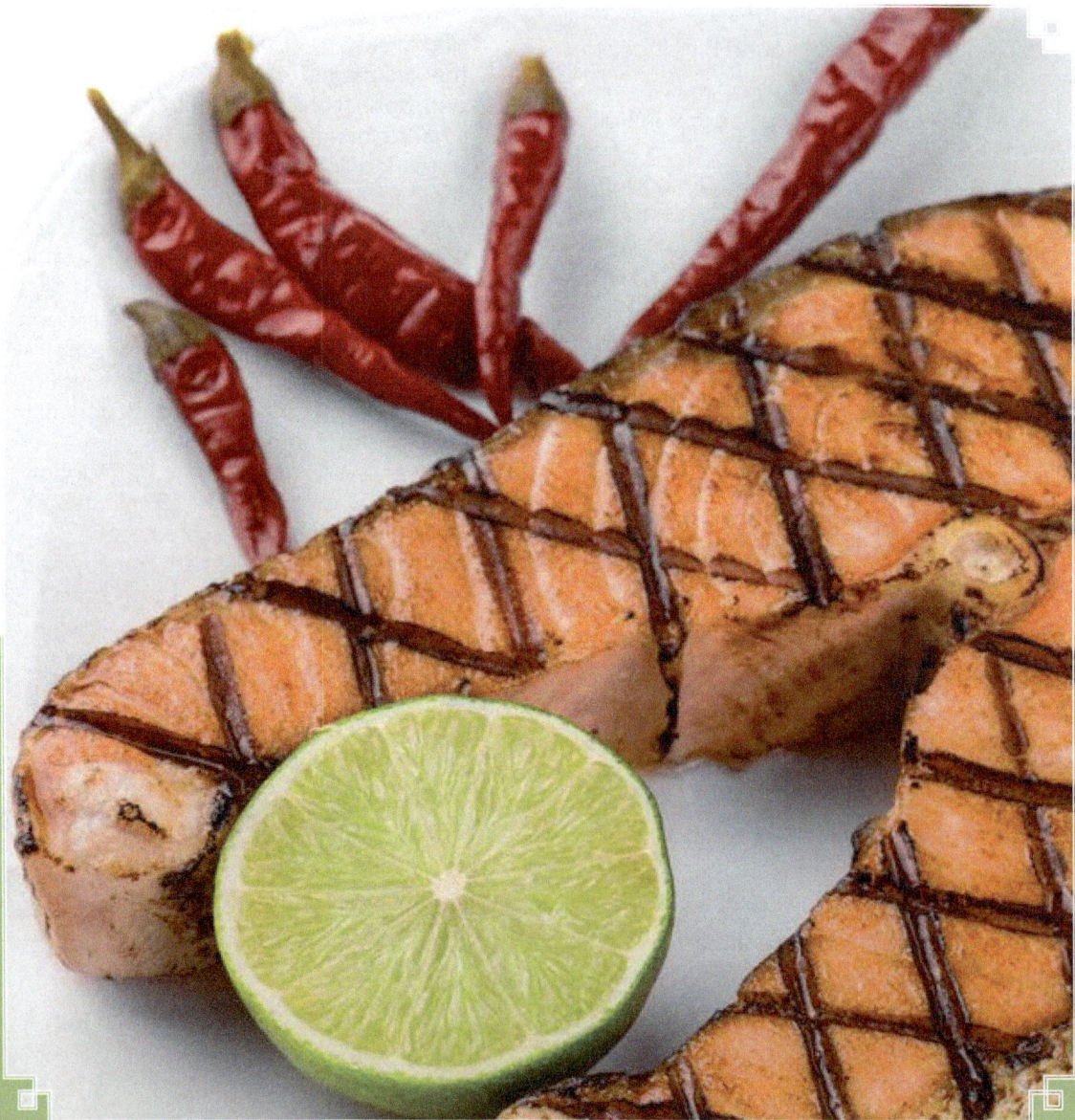

Broiled Grape Leaf–Wrapped Grouper

Prep time: 5 minutes | Cook time: 30 minutes | Serves 4

- 3 tablespoons extra-virgin olive oil, plus extra for brushing
- 2 tablespoons minced fresh parsley
- 1 tablespoon capers, rinsed and minced
- 1 teaspoon grated lemon zest
- ½ teaspoon salt
- ½ teaspoon pepper
- 4 (4- to 6-ounce) skinless grouper fillets, ¾ to 1 inch thick
- 1 (16-ounce) jar grape leaves
- ½ cup Tahini-Lemon Dressing

1. Whisk oil, parsley, capers, lemon zest, salt, and pepper together in medium bowl. Add grouper and gently turn to coat. Cover and refrigerate while preparing grape leaves.
2. Reserve 24 intact grape leaves, roughly 6 inches in diameter; set aside remaining leaves for another use. Bring 8 cups water to boil in large saucepan. Add grape leaves and cook for 5 minutes. Gently drain leaves and transfer to bowl of cold water to cool, about 5 minutes. Drain again thoroughly.
3. Adjust oven rack 8 inches from broiler element and heat broiler. Set wire rack in rimmed baking sheet and spray with vegetable oil spray. Shingle 5 leaves smooth side down on counter into 9-inch circle with stems pointing toward center of circle, then place 1 leaf smooth side down over opening in center. Place 1 fillet in center of leaf circle and spoon portion of remaining marinade on top. Fold sides of leaf circle over grouper, then fold up bottom of circle and continue to roll tightly into packet. Transfer packet seam side down to prepared rack. Repeat with remaining grape leaves, fillets, and marinade.
4. Pat tops of grouper packets dry with paper towels and brush with extra oil.

Broil until grape leaves are crisp and lightly charred and grouper registers 140 degrees, 12 to 18 minutes, rotating sheet halfway through broiling. Serve with Tahini-Lemon Dressing.

Tuna Veggie

Prep time: 5 minutes | Cook time: 12 minutes | Serves 4

- 1 red bell pepper, chopped
- 1 cup green beans, cut into 2-inch pieces
- 2 tablespoons low-sodium soy sauce
- 1 onion, sliced
- 2 cloves garlic, sliced
- 1 tablespoon honey
- 225g fresh tuna, cubed

1. In a 6-inch metal bowl, combine the rapeseed oil, onion, red bell pepper, green beans, and garlic.
2. Pour the mixture into the basket of the Air Fryer. Set the temperature to 175°C (350°F), and cook for 6 minutes, stirring once during cooking, until the vegetables are crisp and tender.
3. Add the honey, low-sodium soy sauce, and tuna to the bowl, and mix everything together.
4. Cook for another 6 minutes, stirring once during cooking, until the tuna is cooked through.
5. Once done, serve your delicious Air Fryer Honey Soy Tuna Stir-Fry over steamed rice or noodles for a tasty and healthy meal. Enjoy!

Provençal Braised Hake

Prep time: 5 minutes | Cook time: 20 minutes | Serves 4

- 2 tablespoons extra-virgin olive oil, plus extra for serving
- 1 onion, halved and sliced thin
- 1 fennel bulb, stalks discarded, bulb halved, cored, and sliced thin
- Salt and pepper to taste
- 4 garlic cloves, minced
- 1 teaspoon minced fresh thyme or ¼ teaspoon dried thyme
- 1 (400g) can diced tomatoes, drained
- 120ml dry white wine
- 4 kinless hake fillets, 1 to 1½ inches thick
- 2 tablespoons minced fresh parsley

1. In a large skillet, heat 2 tablespoons of extra-virgin olive oil over medium heat. Add the sliced onion and fennel, and season with ½ teaspoon of salt and pepper. Cook, stirring occasionally, until the vegetables are softened, which should take about 5 minutes.
2. Stir in the minced garlic and fresh thyme, and cook for an additional 30 seconds until fragrant.
3. Stir in the drained diced tomatoes and dry white wine, and bring the mixture to a simmer.
4. Pat the hake fillets dry with paper towels, then season them with salt and pepper. Nestle the hake fillets skinned side down into the skillet, spooning some of the sauce over the top. Bring the mixture to a simmer, then reduce the heat to medium-low, cover the skillet, and cook the hake for 10 to 12 minutes, or until the fish flakes apart when gently prodded with a paring knife and reaches an internal temperature of 140 degrees Fahrenheit.
5. Carefully transfer the hake fillets to individual shallow bowls.
6. Stir the minced parsley into the sauce, and season with salt and pepper to taste.
7. Spoon the sauce over the hake fillets, drizzle with extra olive oil, and serve.

Cilantro-Lime Fried Shrimp

Prep time: 10 minutes | Cook time: 10 minutes | Serves 4

- 450g raw prawns, peeled and deveined with tails on or off
- 120ml chopped fresh coriander (cilantro)
- Juice of 1 lime
- 1 egg
- 65g plain flour
- 90g bread crumbs
- Salt and pepper to taste
- Cooking spray or oil
- 120ml cocktail sauce (for serving)

1. Place the prawns in a plastic bag and add the chopped coriander and lime juice. Seal the bag and shake it to ensure the prawns are coated with the marinade. Marinate the prawns in the refrigerator for 30 minutes.
2. In three separate small bowls, set up your breading station. Beat the egg in one bowl. Place the flour in another bowl. In the third bowl, mix the bread crumbs with a pinch of salt and pepper.
3. Preheat your Air Fryer to 200°C (400°F).
4. Spray the Air Fryer basket with cooking spray or lightly brush it with oil.
5. Remove the prawns from the marinade, allowing any excess liquid to drain off. Dip each prawn into the flour, then the beaten egg, and finally coat it in the seasoned bread crumbs, pressing gently to adhere the crumbs to the prawns.
6. Arrange the breaded prawns in a single layer in the Air Fryer basket.
7. Lightly spray the prawns with cooking spray or brush them with oil.
8. Cook the prawns in the Air Fryer for 4 minutes, then open the Air Fryer and flip the prawns to ensure even cooking.
9. Cook the prawns for an additional 4 minutes, or until they are crispy and golden brown.
10. Once done, remove the prawns from the Air Fryer and let them cool slightly.

Pan-Roasted Sea Bass with Wild Mushrooms

Prep time: 5 minutes | Cook time: 30 minutes | Serves 4

- 120ml water
- 9g dried porcini mushrooms
- 4 (4- to 6-ounce) skinless sea bass fillets, 1 to 1½ inches thick
- 60ml extra virgin olive oil, plus extra for serving
- Salt and pepper to taste
- 1 sprig fresh rosemary
- 1 red onion, halved and sliced thin
- 340g portobello mushroom caps, halved and sliced 1 cm thick
- 454g cremini mushrooms, trimmed and halved if small or quartered if large
- 2 garlic cloves, minced
- 1 tablespoon minced fresh parsley
- Lemon wedges for serving

1. In a microwave-safe bowl, microwave 120ml of water and dried porcini mushrooms for about 1 minute until steaming. Let the mushrooms sit in the water until softened, which should take about 5 minutes. Drain the mushrooms in a fine-mesh strainer lined with a coffee filter, reserving the porcini liquid. Mince the softened porcini mushrooms and set them aside.
2. Preheat the oven to 245°C. Adjust the oven rack to the lower-middle position.
3. Pat the sea bass fillets dry with paper towels, then rub them with 2 tablespoons of olive oil, and season them with salt and pepper.
4. In a 12-inch oven-safe skillet, heat the remaining 2 tablespoons of olive oil and the sprig of rosemary over medium-high heat until shimmering. Add the sliced red onion, portobello mushrooms, cremini mushrooms, and ½ teaspoon of salt. Cook, stirring occasionally, until the mushrooms have released their liquid and are beginning to brown, which should take about 8 to 10 minutes. Stir in the minced garlic and the minced porcini mushrooms, and cook until fragrant, about 30 seconds.
5. Off the heat, stir in the reserved porcini liquid. Nestle the sea bass fillets skinned side down into the skillet. Transfer the skillet to the preheated oven and roast until the fish flakes apart when gently prodded with a paring knife and reaches an internal temperature of 140 degrees Fahrenheit, which should take about 10 to 12 minutes.
6. Sprinkle the British-Style Roasted Sea Bass and Mushroom Medley with minced fresh parsley and drizzle with some extra virgin olive oil.
7. Serve the sea bass and mushroom medley with lemon wedges on the side

Creole Crayfish

Prep time: 10 minutes | cook time:3 to 4 hours |Serves 2

- 1.5 cups diced celery
- 1 large yellow onion, chopped
- 2 small bell peppers, any colors, chopped
- 1 250g can tomato sauce
- 1 400g can whole tomatoes, broken up, with the juice
- 1 garlic clove, minced
- 1 teaspoon sea salt
- ¼ teaspoon black pepper
- 6 drops hot pepper sauce (like Tabasco)
- 450g precooked crayfish meat

1. Place the celery, onion, and bell peppers in the slow cooker.
2. Add the tomato sauce, whole tomatoes, garlic, salt, pepper, and hot sauce.
3. Cover and cook on high for 3 to 4 hours or on low for 6 to 8 hours, or until the vegetables are tender.
4. About 30 minutes before the cooking time is completed, add the crayfish.
5. Serve hot.

Garlicky Roasted Shrimp with Parsley and Anise

Prep time: 5 minutes | Cook time: 25 minutes | Serves 4-6

- 60ml salt
- 2 pounds shell-on jumbo shrimp (16 to 20 per pound)
- 60ml extra-virgin olive oil
- 6 garlic cloves, minced
- 1 teaspoon anise seeds
- ½ teaspoon red pepper flakes
- ¼ teaspoon black pepper
- 2 tablespoons minced fresh parsley
- Lemon wedges for serving

1. In a large bowl, dissolve ¼ cup of salt in cold water. Add the jumbo shrimp to the bowl and let them soak in the brine for about 15 minutes. This will help the shrimp stay tender and flavorful during cooking.
2. After the brining time, drain the shrimp and pat them dry with paper towels.
3. In a large skillet, heat the extra-virgin olive oil over medium heat. Add the minced garlic, anise seeds, red pepper flakes, and black pepper. Cook, stirring constantly, until the garlic becomes fragrant, which should take about 30 seconds to 1 minute.
4. Add the jumbo shrimp to the skillet and cook them, stirring occasionally, until they turn pink and are just cooked through. Be careful not to overcook the shrimp to keep them tender and juicy.
5. Sprinkle the minced fresh parsley over the British-Style Spiced Shrimp and toss them to combine with the flavorful oil and spices.
6. Serve the spiced shrimp with lemon wedges on the side for squeezing over the shrimp.

Steamed Mediterranean Cod

Prep time: 5 minutes | Cook time: 20 minutes | Serves 4

- 454g cherry tomatoes, halved
- 1 bunch fresh thyme sprigs
- 4 fillets of cod
- 5ml olive oil
- 1 clove garlic, pressed
- 3 pinches of salt
- 480ml water
- 240g white rice
- 150g Kalamata olives
- 30ml pickled capers
- 15ml olive oil
- 1 pinch ground black pepper

1. Line a parchment paper on the basket of your Instant Pot. Place about half the tomatoes in a single layer on the paper. Sprinkle with thyme, reserving some for garnish.
2. Arrange cod fillets on top. Sprinkle with a little bit of olive oil.
3. Spread the garlic, pepper, salt, and remaining tomatoes over the fish. In the pot, mix rice and water.
4. Lay a trivet over the rice and water. Lower steamer basket onto the trivet.
5. Seal the lid, and cook for 7 minutes on Low Pressure. Quick release the pressure.
6. Remove the steamer basket and trivet from the pot. Use a fork to fluff rice.
7. Plate the fish fillets and apply a garnish of olives, reserved thyme, pepper, remaining olive oil, and capers. Serve with rice.

Endive with Shrimp

Prep time: 5 minutes | Cook time: 15 minutes | Serves 4

- 60ml olive oil
- 1 small shallot, minced
- 1 tablespoon Dijon mustard
- Juice and zest of 1 lemon
- Sea salt and freshly ground pepper, to taste
- 480ml salted water
- 14 shrimp, peeled and deveined
- 1 head endive
- 120g tart green apple, diced
- 30g toasted walnuts

1. For the vinaigrette, whisk together the first five ingredients in a small bowl until creamy and emulsified.
2. Refrigerate for at least 2 hours for the best flavor.
3. In a small pan, boil salted water. Add the shrimp and cook 1–2 minutes, or until the shrimp turns pink. Drain and cool under cold water.
4. To assemble the salad, wash and break the endive. Place on serving plates and top with the shrimp, green apple, and toasted walnuts.
5. Drizzle with the vinaigrette before serving.

Burgundy Salmon

Prep time: 5 minutes | Cook time: 15 minutes | Serves 4

- 4 salmon fillets
- Sea salt and freshly ground pepper, to taste
- 1 tablespoon olive oil
- 1 shallot, minced
- 480 ml high-quality Burgundy wine
- 120 ml beef stock
- 2 tablespoons tomato paste
- 1 teaspoon fresh thyme, chopped

1. Preheat the oven to 350 degrees Fahrenheit (approximately 175 degrees Celsius).
2. Season the salmon fillets with sea salt and freshly ground pepper to taste. Wrap each salmon fillet individually in aluminum foil and bake for 10–13 minutes until the salmon is cooked through.
3. In a deep skillet, heat the olive oil over medium heat. Add the minced shallot and cook for about 3 minutes or until tender.
4. Pour in the Burgundy wine, beef stock, and tomato paste. Simmer the sauce for 10 minutes or until it thickens and reduces by about one-third.
5. Place the baked salmon fillets on a serving platter and spoon the Burgundy sauce over them.

Shrimp with Marinara Sauce

Prep time: 5 minutes | Cook time:6 to 7 hours 15 hours |Serves 4

- 170g tomato paste (6-ounce can)
- 1 clove garlic, minced
- 2 tablespoons minced fresh flat-leaf parsley
- ½ teaspoon dried basil
- 1 teaspoon dried oregano
- 1 teaspoon garlic powder
- 1½ teaspoons sea salt
- ¼ teaspoon black pepper
- 450g cooked shrimp, peeled and deveined
- 400g hot cooked spaghetti or linguine, for serving
- 55g grated Parmesan cheese, for serving

1. Combine the tomato paste, minced garlic, minced parsley, dried basil, dried oregano, garlic powder, sea salt, and black pepper in the slow cooker.
2. Stir well to ensure the mixture is evenly combined.
3. Cover and cook on low for 6 to 7 hours.
4. Turn up the heat to high, stir in the cooked shrimp, and cover and cook on high for about 15 minutes longer.
5. Serve hot over the cooked pasta. Top with grated Parmesan cheese.

Chapter 10

Vegetables and Vegan

Braised Cauliflower with Garlic and White Wine

Prep time: 5 minutes | Cook time: 15 minutes | Serves 4-6

- 4 tablespoons extra-virgin olive oil
- 3 garlic cloves, minced
- ⅛ teaspoon red pepper flakes
- 1 head cauliflower (2 pounds), cored and cut into 1½-inch florets
- Salt and pepper to taste
- 80ml chicken or vegetable broth
- 80ml dry white wine
- 2 tablespoons minced fresh parsley

1. In a small bowl, combine 1 teaspoon of olive oil with minced garlic and red pepper flakes.
2. In a 12-inch skillet, heat the remaining 3 tablespoons of olive oil over medium-high heat until shimmering. Add the cauliflower florets and ¼ teaspoon of salt. Sauté the cauliflower, stirring occasionally, until the florets are golden brown, which should take about 7 to 9 minutes.
3. Push the cauliflower to the sides of the skillet, creating a space in the center. Add the garlic mixture to the center and cook, mashing the mixture into the skillet until it becomes fragrant, about 30 seconds. Stir the garlic mixture into the cauliflower.
4. Stir in the chicken or vegetable broth and dry white wine, and bring the mixture to a simmer. Reduce the heat to medium-low, cover the skillet, and cook until the cauliflower is crisp-tender, which should take about 4 to 6 minutes.
5. Off the heat, stir in the minced fresh parsley and season the British Sautéed Cauliflower with Garlic and Parsley with salt and pepper to taste.
6. Serve the cauliflower as a delicious and flavorful side dish or a light main course.

Herby-Garlic Potatoes

Prep time: 5 minutes | Cook time: 30 minutes | Serves 4

- 680 grams potatoes
- 3 tablespoons butter
- 3 cloves garlic, thinly chopped
- 2 tablespoons fresh rosemary, chopped
- ½ teaspoon fresh thyme, chopped
- ½ teaspoon fresh parsley, chopped
- ¼ teaspoon ground black pepper
- 120ml vegetable broth

1. Peel and cut the potatoes into bite-sized pieces.
2. In the instant pot, melt the butter on Sauté mode. Add the chopped garlic, rosemary, thyme, parsley, and black pepper. Cook for a few minutes until the mixture becomes aromatic.
3. Add the potato pieces to the pot and stir to coat them with the herb mixture.
4. Pour in the vegetable broth and give it a quick stir to combine.
5. Seal the lid and set the instant pot to Pressure Cook mode for 5 minutes on High Pressure.
6. Once the cooking is done, do a quick pressure release.
7. Carefully open the lid and give the potatoes a gentle stir before serving.

Grilled Aubergine with Yogurt Sauce

Prep time: 5 minutes | Cook time: 10 minutes | Serves 4-6

- 6 tablespoons extra-virgin olive oil
- 5 garlic cloves, minced
- 1/8 teaspoon red pepper flakes
- 120 ml plain whole-milk yogurt
- 3 tablespoons chopped fresh mint
- 1 teaspoon grated lemon zest plus 2 teaspoons juice
- 1 teaspoon ground cumin
- Salt and pepper
- 900 grams aubergine, sliced into 6mm-thick rounds

1. Combine extra-virgin olive oil, minced garlic, and red pepper flakes in a bowl. Microwave until garlic is golden brown and crisp, about 2 minutes. Strain the garlic oil through a fine-mesh strainer into a small bowl. Reserve the garlic oil and garlic separately.
2. Whisk 1 tablespoon of the garlic oil with yogurt, chopped fresh mint, grated lemon zest, lemon juice, ground cumin, and ¼ teaspoon of salt in a separate bowl. Set aside for serving.
3. For a charcoal grill: Open the bottom vent completely. Light a large chimney starter filled with charcoal briquettes (around 6 quarts). When the top coals are partially covered with ash, pour them evenly over the grill. Set the cooking grate in place, cover, and open the lid vent completely. Heat the grill until hot, about 5 minutes.
4. For a gas grill: Turn all burners to high, cover, and heat the grill until hot, about 15 minutes. Then, turn all burners to medium-high.
5. Clean and oil the cooking grate. Brush the aubergine slices with the remaining garlic oil and season them with salt and pepper. Place half of the aubergine on the grill and cook (covered if using a gas grill) until browned and tender, about 4 minutes per side. Transfer the grilled aubergine to a serving platter. Repeat with the remaining aubergine slices and transfer them to the platter.
6. Drizzle the yogurt sauce over the grilled aubergine and sprinkle with the reserved garlic (the one set aside from the garlic oil). Serve.

Greek-Style Garlic-Lemon Potatoes

Prep time:5 minutes | Cook time: 25 minutes | Serves 4-6

- 45ml (3½ tablespoons) extra-virgin olive oil, plus more for drizzling
- 750g (1½lb) Yukon Gold potatoes, peeled and cut lengthwise into ¾-inch-thick wedges
- 2 tablespoons minced fresh oregano
- 6 garlic cloves, minced
- 2 teaspoons grated lemon zest plus 3 tablespoons juice
- Salt and pepper
- 2 tablespoons minced fresh parsley

1. Heat 30ml (2 tablespoons) of the olive oil in a large non-stick frying pan over a medium-high heat. Add the potatoes cut side down in a single layer and cook until golden brown on first side (the pan should sizzle but not smoke), about 6 minutes. Using tongs, flip the potatoes onto their second cut side and cook until golden brown, about 5 minutes. Reduce the heat to medium-low, cover, and cook until the potatoes are tender, 8-12 minutes.
2. Meanwhile, whisk the remaining 15ml (1 tablespoon) olive oil, oregano, garlic, lemon zest and juice, ½ teaspoon salt, and ½ teaspoon pepper together in a small bowl. When the potatoes are tender, gently stir in the garlic mixture and cook, uncovered, until fragrant, about 2 minutes. Off the heat, gently stir in the parsley and season with salt and pepper to taste. Serve drizzled with extra olive oil.

Zucchini and Feta Fritters

Prep time:5 minutes | Cook time: 15 minutes | Serves 4-6

- 500g (1lb) zucchini, grated
- Salt and pepper
- 115g (4oz) feta cheese, crumbled
- 2 spring onions, finely chopped
- 2 large eggs, beaten
- 2 tablespoons chopped fresh dill
- 1 garlic clove, minced
- 50g (1/4 cup) all-purpose flour
- 180ml (6fl oz) extra-virgin olive oil
- Lemon wedges

1. Preheat the oven to 200°C (400°F). Toss the zucchini with 1 teaspoon salt and let drain in a fine-mesh sieve for 10 minutes.
2. Wrap the zucchini in a clean dish towel and squeeze out as much liquid as possible. Transfer to a large bowl and stir in the feta, spring onions, eggs, dill, garlic, and ¼ teaspoon pepper. Sprinkle in the flour and stir to incorporate.
3. Heat 45ml (3½ tablespoons) of the olive oil in a large non-stick frying pan over a medium heat until shimmering. Drop 2 tablespoons of batter into the pan and use the back of a spoon to press it into a 2-inch-wide fritter (you should be able to fit about 6 fritters in the pan at a time). Fry for 3 minutes per side, or until golden brown.
4. Transfer the fritters to a paper towel-lined baking sheet and keep warm in the oven. Wipe the pan clean with paper towels and repeat with the remaining 45ml (3½ tablespoons) olive oil and remaining batter. Serve with lemon wedges.

Vibrant Green Beans

Prep time: 5 minutes | Cook time: 15 minutes | Serves 6

- 30ml olive oil
- 2 leeks, white parts only, sliced
- Sea salt and freshly ground pepper, to taste
- 450g fresh green string beans, trimmed
- 1 tablespoon Italian seasoning
- 30ml white wine
- Zest of 1 lemon

1. Heat the olive oil over medium heat in a large skillet.
2. Add the sliced leeks and cook, stirring often, until they start to brown and become lightly caramelized.
3. Season the leeks with sea salt and freshly ground pepper to taste.
4. Add the fresh green string beans and Italian seasoning to the skillet. Cook for a few minutes until the beans are tender but still crisp to the bite.
5. Pour the white wine into the skillet and continue cooking until the green beans are done to your liking and the leeks are crispy and browned.
6. Sprinkle the dish with lemon zest before serving to add a refreshing citrus flavor.
7. Serve the delicious and flavorful leeks and green beans as a side dish to complement your main course.

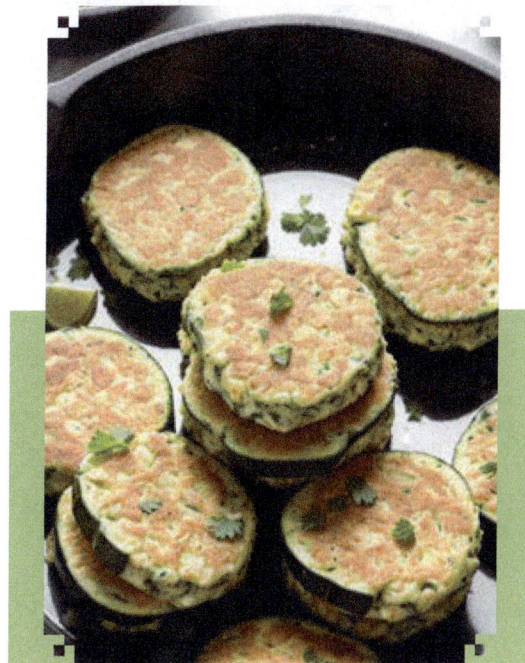

Roasted Green Beans with Pecorino and Pine Nuts

Prep time: 5 minutes | Cook time: 25 minutes | Serves 4-6

- 680g green beans, trimmed
- 60ml extra-virgin olive oil
- ¾ teaspoon sugar
- Salt and pepper to taste
- 2 garlic cloves, minced
- 1 teaspoon grated lemon zest plus 1 tablespoon lemon juice
- 1 teaspoon Dijon mustard
- 2 tablespoons chopped fresh basil
- 60g shredded Pecorino Romano cheese
- 2 tablespoons toasted pine nuts

1. Adjust the oven rack to the lowest position and preheat the oven to 240°C.
2. Toss the green beans with 1 tablespoon of olive oil, sugar, ¼ teaspoon of salt, and ½ teaspoon of pepper. Transfer the seasoned green beans to a rimmed baking sheet and spread them into a single layer.
3. Cover the baking sheet tightly with aluminum foil and roast the green beans for 10 minutes. Then, remove the foil and continue to roast until the green beans become spotty brown, about 10 more minutes, stirring halfway through roasting.
4. While the green beans are roasting, combine the minced garlic, grated lemon zest, and remaining 3 tablespoons of olive oil in a medium bowl. Microwave the mixture until it begins to bubble, which should take about 1 minute. Let the mixture steep for 1 minute, then whisk in the lemon juice, Dijon mustard, ⅛ teaspoon of salt, and ¼ teaspoon of pepper until the dressing is well combined.
5. Once the green beans are roasted, transfer them to the bowl with the lemon basil dressing. Add the chopped fresh basil and toss the green beans to combine with the dressing and basil.
6. Season the British Roasted Green Beans with Lemon Basil Dressing with salt and pepper to taste.
7. Transfer the dressed green beans to a serving platter and sprinkle the shredded Pecorino Romano cheese and toasted pine nuts over them.
8. Serve the green beans as a delightful and flavorful side dish.

Sautéed Spinach with Yogurt and Dukkah

Prep time:5 minutes | Cook time: 20 minutes | Serves 4

- 125ml (½ cup) plain yogurt
- 2 teaspoons grated lemon zest plus 1 teaspoon juice
- 45ml (3½ tablespoons) extra-virgin olive oil
- 600g (20oz) curly-leaf spinach, stemmed
- 4 garlic cloves, minced
- Salt and pepper
- 75g (¼ cup) dukkah

1. Combine the yogurt, lemon zest and juice in a bowl; set aside for serving. Heat 15ml (1 tablespoon) of the olive oil in a large Dutch oven over a high heat until shimmering. Add the spinach, 1 handful at a time, stirring and tossing each handful to wilt slightly before adding more. Cook the spinach, stirring constantly, until uniformly wilted, about 1 minute. Transfer the spinach to a colander and squeeze between tongs to release excess liquid.
2. Wipe the pot dry with paper towels. Add the remaining 30ml (2 tablespoons) olive oil and garlic to the now-empty pot and cook over a medium heat until fragrant, about 30 seconds. Add the spinach and toss to coat, gently separating the leaves to evenly coat with the garlic oil. Off the heat, season with salt and pepper to taste. Transfer the spinach to a serving platter, drizzle with the yogurt sauce, and sprinkle with the dukkah. Serve.

Braised Aubergine and Tomatoes

Prep time: 5 minutes | Cook time: 15 minutes | Serves 4

- 1 large aubergine (aubergine), peeled and diced
- Pinch of sea salt
- 1 (400g) can chopped tomatoes and their juices
- 240ml chicken or vegetable broth
- 2 garlic cloves, smashed
- 1 tablespoon dried Italian herbs (such as oregano, thyme, or basil)
- 1 bay leaf
- Sea salt and freshly ground pepper, to taste

1. Cut the aubergine (aubergine) into cubes and sprinkle a pinch of sea salt on both sides of each piece. Let the aubergine sit for about 20 minutes to allow any bitter juices to be released. Afterward, rinse the aubergine thoroughly and pat it dry with paper towels.
2. Dice the prepared aubergine into smaller pieces.
3. In a large saucepot, combine the diced aubergine, chopped tomatoes and their juices, chicken or vegetable broth, smashed garlic cloves, dried Italian herbs, and the bay leaf.
4. Bring the mixture to a boil and then reduce the heat to a simmer.
5. Cover the pot and let it simmer for about 30–40 minutes or until the aubergine is tender.
6. Remove the garlic cloves and bay leaf from the pot. Season the braised aubergine and tomatoes with sea salt and freshly ground pepper according to your taste preferences.
7. Serve the delicious British version of Braised Aubergine and Tomatoes.

Greek Stewed Zucchini

Prep time: 5 minutes | Cook time:40 minutes |Serves 4 to 6

- 60ml extra-virgin olive oil
- 1 small yellow onion, peeled and thinly sliced
- 4 medium courgettes (zucchini), cut into 1 cm-thick rounds
- 4 small garlic cloves, minced
- 1 to 2 teaspoons dried oregano
- 400g chopped tomatoes
- 100g halved and pitted Kalamata olives
- 75g crumbled feta cheese
- 15g chopped fresh flat-leaf parsley, for garnish (optional)

1. In a large skillet, heat the oil over medium-high heat. Add the thinly sliced onion and sauté until just tender, 6 to 8 minutes. Add the courgettes, garlic, and oregano and sauté another 6 to 8 minutes, or until the courgettes are just tender.
2. Add the chopped tomatoes and bring to a boil. Reduce the heat to low and add the olives. Cover and simmer on low heat for 20 minutes, or until the flavors have developed and the courgettes are very tender.
3. Serve warm topped with feta and parsley (if using).

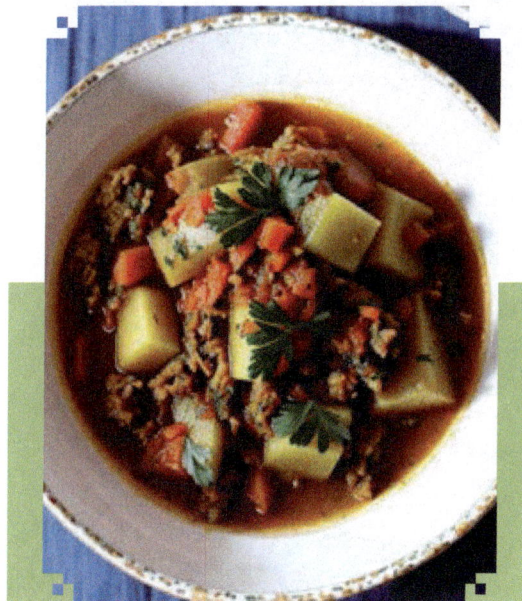

Chapter 11

Desserts

Pumpkin & Walnut Sweet Rolls

Prep time: 5 minutes | Cook time: 30 minutes | Serves 8

- 480ml pumpkin puree
- 1 tsp vanilla extract
- 480ml Greek yogurt
- 2 eggs
- 2 tbsp brown sugar
- 2 tbsp unsalted butter, softened
- 2 puff pastry sheets
- 120g walnuts, chopped

1. In a bowl, mix Greek yogurt with vanilla extract until completely smooth; set aside.
2. Unfold the pastry and cut each sheet into 10cm x 18cm pieces and brush with half of the beaten eggs. Place approximately 2 tbsp of pumpkin puree and 2 tbsp of the yogurt mixture in the middle of each pastry. Sprinkle with chopped walnuts.
3. Fold the sheets over the filling to create strudels, and brush the surface with the remaining beaten eggs. Cut a few slits on the top to allow steam to escape.
4. Pour 240ml of water into the instant pot and insert the trivet. Place the baking dish with the strudels on top of the trivet. Seal the lid and cook for 25 minutes on High Pressure.
5. Allow the pressure to release naturally for about 10 minutes, then carefully remove the lid. Let the strudels cool for 10 minutes before transferring them to a serving plate.

Dolmades

Prep time: 5 minutes | Cook time: 15 minutes | Serves 6

- 15ml olive oil
- 3 shallots, chopped
- 2 cloves garlic, minced
- 180g short-grain rice
- 40g golden raisins
- 40g pine nuts, toasted
- Juice of 1 lemon
- Sea salt and freshly ground pepper, to taste
- 160ml water
- 4 spring onions, chopped
- 1 small bunch mint leaves, finely chopped
- 1 small bunch flat-leaf parsley, chopped
- 20 preserved grape leaves

1. Heat the olive oil in a large skillet over medium heat. Add the chopped shallots and minced garlic, and sauté for 5 minutes until softened.
2. Stir in the short-grain rice, golden raisins, toasted pine nuts, and lemon juice. Season with sea salt and freshly ground pepper according to taste.
3. Pour in 160ml of water, bring to a boil, then cover the skillet with a lid. Reduce the heat to low, and let the rice simmer for about 20 minutes or until it's cooked and the liquid is absorbed.
4. Turn off the heat and allow the rice to cool.
5. Add the chopped spring onions, mint leaves, and flat-leaf parsley to the rice filling. Mix well to combine all the ingredients.
6. Rinse the preserved grape leaves under cold water to remove any excess brine. Pat them dry with a paper towel.
7. Place about 1 tablespoon of the rice filling in the center of each grape leaf, then roll it tightly to form a neat package with the seam side down.
8. Arrange the stuffed grape leaves in a steamer, and steam for about 10 minutes or until the leaves are tender.
9. Serve the stuffed grape leaves warm as a delicious appetizer or side dish.

Vanilla Bites

Prep time: 10 minutes | Cook time: 45 minutes | Makes 24 bites

- 340g (12-ounce) box butter cake mix
- 115g (1 stick) butter, melted
- 2 large eggs, divided
- 200g sugar
- 225g (8-ounce) package cream cheese, softened
- 1 teaspoon vanilla extract

1. Preheat the oven to 350°F (175°C). Grease and flour a 9x13-inch baking pan or line it with parchment paper, then set it aside.
2. To make the first layer, in a medium bowl, combine the butter cake mix, melted butter, and 1 egg. Mix well until a soft dough forms. Press the dough evenly into the bottom of the prepared baking pan.
3. In another bowl, make the second layer by mixing together the sugar, softened cream cheese, the remaining 2 eggs, and vanilla extract until smooth and well combined.
4. Gently pour the cream cheese mixture over the first layer in the baking pan, spreading it evenly to cover the cake layer.
5. Bake the Vanilla Bites in the preheated oven for 45 to 50 minutes or until the top is lightly golden and the center is set. Allow the bites to cool completely in the pan on a wire rack.
6. Once cooled, cut the cake into 24 small squares to create the bites.

Avocado-Orange Fruit Salad

Prep time: 10 minutes | Cook time: 15 minutes | Serves 4

- 2 large Gala apples, chopped
- 2 oranges, segmented and chopped
- ⅓ cup sliced almonds
- 5ml honey
- 10ml extra-virgin olive oil
- ½ teaspoon grated orange zest

- 1 large avocado, semi-ripened, medium diced

1. In a large bowl, combine the apples, oranges, and almonds. Mix gently.
2. In a small bowl, whisk the honey, oil, and orange zest. Set aside.
3. Drizzle the orange zest mix over the fruit salad and toss. Add the avocado and toss gently one more time.

Individual Apple Pockets

Prep time: 5 minutes | Cook time: 15 minutes | Serves 6

- 1 sheet of organic puff pastry, rolled out and at room temperature
- 1 Gala apple, peeled and sliced
- 60g brown sugar
- 50mg ground cinnamon
- 50mg ground cardamom
- Nonstick cooking spray
- Honey, for topping

1. Preheat the oven to 350°F.
2. Cut the pastry dough into 4 even discs. Peel and slice the apple. In a small bowl, toss the slices with brown sugar, cinnamon, and cardamom.
3. Spray a muffin tin very well with nonstick cooking spray. Be sure to spray only the muffin holders you plan to use.
4. Once sprayed, line the bottom of the muffin tin with the dough and place 1 or 2 broken apple slices on top. Fold the remaining dough over the apple and drizzle with honey.
5. Bake for 15 minutes or until brown and bubbly.

Ricotta-Lemon Cheesecake

Prep time: 5 minutes | Cook time: 1 hour | Serves 8-10

- 2 (225g) packages full-fat cream cheese
- 1 (450g) container full-fat ricotta cheese
- 300g caster sugar (fine granulated sugar)
- Zest of 1 lemon
- 5 large eggs
- Nonstick cooking spray

1. Preheat the oven to 180°C.
2. Using a mixer, blend together the full-fat cream cheese and ricotta cheese until smooth and well combined.
3. Blend in the caster sugar and lemon zest until the mixture is creamy and evenly mixed.
4. One at a time, blend in the large eggs, dropping in one egg at a time. Blend for about 10 seconds after each addition to ensure thorough mixing.
5. Line a 23cm (9-inch) springform pan with parchment paper and lightly grease it with nonstick cooking spray.
6. Pour the cheesecake batter into the prepared pan.
7. To create a water bath, place the springform pan into a larger baking or roasting pan. Fill the larger pan about ⅓ of the way up with warm water.
8. Put the whole setup in the preheated oven and bake the cheesecake for about 1 hour, or until the edges are set and the center is slightly jiggly.
9. Once the baking is complete, remove the cheesecake from the water bath and carefully remove the foil from the bottom of the pan.
10. Allow the cheesecake to cool at room temperature for about 1 hour, then refrigerate it for at least 3 hours before serving.

Lemon Cookies

Prep time: 10 minutes | Cook time: 10 minutes | Serves 12

- Nonstick cooking spray

- 150g granulated sugar
- 115g butter, softened
- 1 ½ teaspoons vinegar
- 1 large egg
- 1 teaspoon grated lemon zest
- 210g all-purpose flour
- 1 teaspoon baking powder
- ¼ teaspoon baking soda
- 90g confectioners' sugar
- 60ml freshly squeezed lemon juice
- 1 teaspoon finely grated lemon zest

1. Preheat the oven to 350° F (175° C). Spray a baking sheet with nonstick cooking spray and set it aside.
2. In a medium bowl, cream together the granulated sugar and softened butter until light and fluffy.
3. Stir in the vinegar, then add the egg and grated lemon zest, mixing well after each addition.
4. Sift the all-purpose flour, baking powder, and baking soda into the bowl with the wet ingredients. Mix until the dry ingredients are fully incorporated into the dough.
5. Spoon the cookie dough onto the prepared baking sheet in 12 equal mounds. Flatten the mounds slightly with the back of a spoon or your fingers to form cookie shapes.
6. Bake the cookies for 10 to 12 minutes or until the edges are lightly golden. Be careful not to overbake to avoid burning the bottoms.
7. While the cookies are baking, prepare the lemon glaze. In a small bowl, whisk together the confectioners' sugar, freshly squeezed lemon juice, and finely grated lemon zest until smooth.
8. Once the cookies are done baking, remove them from the oven and let them cool on the baking sheet for a few minutes.
9. Brush the lemon glaze over the warm cookies using a pastry brush or spoon.
10. Allow the glazed cookies to cool completely on a wire rack before serving.

Appendix 1 Measurement Conversion Chart

Volume Equivalents (Dry)

US STANDARD	METRIC (APPROXIMATE)
1/8 teaspoon	0.5 mL
1/4 teaspoon	1 mL
1/2 teaspoon	2 mL
3/4 teaspoon	4 mL
1 teaspoon	5 mL
1 tablespoon	15 mL
1/4 cup	59 mL
1/2 cup	118 mL
3/4 cup	177 mL
1 cup	235 mL
2 cups	475 mL
3 cups	700 mL
4 cups	1 L

Volume Equivalents (Liquid)

US STANDARD	US STANDARD (OUNCES)	METRIC (APPROXIMATE)
2 tablespoons	1 fl.oz.	30 mL
1/4 cup	2 fl.oz.	60 mL
1/2 cup	4 fl.oz.	120 mL
1 cup	8 fl.oz.	240 mL
1 1/2 cup	12 fl.oz.	355 mL
2 cups or 1 pint	16 fl.oz.	475 mL
4 cups or 1 quart	32 fl.oz.	1 L
1 gallon	128 fl.oz.	4 L

Temperatures Equivalents

FAHRENHEIT(F)	CELSIUS(C) APPROXIMATE)
225 °F	107 °C
250 °F	120 ° °C
275 °F	135 °C
300 °F	150 °C
325 °F	160 °C
350 °F	180 °C
375 °F	190 °C
400 °F	205 °C
425 °F	220 °C
450 °F	235 °C
475 °F	245 °C
500 °F	260 °C

Weight Equivalents

US STANDARD	METRIC (APPROXIMATE)
1 ounce	28 g
2 ounces	57 g
5 ounces	142 g
10 ounces	284 g
15 ounces	425 g
16 ounces (1 pound)	455 g
1.5 pounds	680 g
2 pounds	907 g

Appendix 2 The Dirty Dozen and Clean Fifteen

The Environmental Working Group (EWG) is a nonprofit, nonpartisan organization dedicated to protecting human health and the environment Its mission is to empower people to live healthier lives in a healthier environment. This organization publishes an annual list of the twelve kinds of produce, in sequence, that have the highest amount of pesticide residue-the Dirty Dozen-as well as a list of the fifteen kinds ofproduce that have the least amount of pesticide residue-the Clean Fifteen.

THE DIRTY DOZEN	
The 2016 Dirty Dozen includes the following produce. These are considered among the year's most important produce to buy organic:	
Strawberries	Spinach
Apples	Tomatoes
Nectarines	Bell peppers
Peaches	Cherry tomatoes
Celery	Cucumbers
Grapes	Kale/collard greens
Cherries	Hot peppers

The Dirty Dozen list contains two additional itemskale/collard greens and hot peppers-because they tend to contain trace levels of highly hazardous pesticides.

THE CLEAN FIFTEEN	
The least critical to buy organically are the Clean Fifteen list. The following are on the 2016 list:	
Avocados	Papayas
Corn	Kiw
Pineapples	Eggplant
Cabbage	Honeydew
Sweet peas	Grapefruit
Onions	Cantaloupe
Asparagus	Cauliflower
Mangos	

Some of the sweet corn sold in the United States are made from genetically engineered (GE) seedstock. Buy organic varieties of these crops to avoid GE produce.

Appendix 3 Index

Virginia A. Evans

Printed in Great Britain
by Amazon